Leave No ANGRY Child Behind

The ABC's of Anger Management for grades K-12

160
Quick Tips
& Strategies

By Anna T. McFadden, Ph.D. & Kathy Cooper, M.S.W

Layout and design by Tonya Daugherty

ISBN—1889636673

Library of Congress Number
2004101794

10 9 8 7 6 5 4 3 2 1
Printed in the United States

PO Box 115 • Chapin, SC 29036
(800) 209-9774 • (803) 345-1070 • Fax (803) 345-0888
yl@sc.rr.com • www.youthlight.com

Acknowledgements

We are grateful to the many people who had a part in the development of this book. Dr. Robert Bowman and Susan Bowman of Developmental Resources and Youthlight, Inc. provided us both the opportunity to research this topic and present it at workshops around the nation. They also encouraged and supported our work on this publication. We are especially indebted to Tom Carr whose work in this area has informed our understanding and who so willingly shared ideas for this book. Jan Farrell, who has presented on the topic of angry students, also provided input. And finally, we remember with gratitude the teachers, counselors, psychologists, social workers, school administrators, school resource officers, and parents from all over the country who enriched our knowledge of best practice in our workshop experiences. This book is dedicated to these people who love and care for the children and young people with whom they work.

Introduction

I n the aftermath of the tragic events of September 11, the United States Congress passed a significant piece of legislation, the No Child Left Behind Act. An important component of this legislation addresses "persistently dangerous schools."

The purpose of this book is to address the issue of the anger that sometimes leads to student violence and persistently dangerous classrooms and schools. We maintain that angry students may be at great risk for being left behind. Our approach to this issue is not about "Band-Aids," but rather about being proactive.

We are especially interested in the ideas of Ross Greene (2001) in *The Explosive Child* who believes that if we look at anger related behavior as attention seeking, stubborn, coercive, or resistant and defiant, we will respond by attempting to show "who is in charge." On the other hand, if we interpret anger related behavior as often unplanned and unintentional, related to delays in development and problems with skills of flexibility and the ability to tolerate frustration, we will respond differently. It all depends on our frame of reference.

This book offers no quick fixes. Instead it represents an attempt to provide teachers, administrators, counselors, resource officers, social workers, psychologists and parents information to examine the underlying causes of student anger as well as to offer a repertoire of activities and suggestions for dealing with such anger in K-12 students. We have created what we hope is a user friendly collection of alphabetized strategies and research summaries.

The purpose and spirit of this book is to, indeed, "Leave No Angry Child Behind."

The ABC's
of
Anger
Management

Abusive Behaviors: Be on the lookout for abusive family relationships in extremely angry students. He/she may have experienced some kind of abuse from a family member and may simply be acting out what he/she has experienced. If you suspect abuse, always report it to the proper authorities. Counseling may be necessary.

Activate a Plan to Deal with Situations that Cause Conflict

• Define who or what makes you angry.

• Choose one of the many strategies in the book and think through how you'll use it. Practice it with a friend.

• Try to think first and remember to begin using the strategy you've practiced before you become too angry.

• Feel good about yourself. You're in control.

Active Listening: Mendler (1992) offers the following suggestion. When a student confronts you (adult) in a power struggle, simply use active listening and repeat what the student says with a neutral voice. For example, if you ask a student to complete a task and the student says that he/she will not complete the task, simply repeat the student's words back to the student. You might respond back to the student by saying, "You said that you will not complete the task, did I get that right?" If other students question you or imply that you are not dealing with the problem, you might tell them that you will be dealing with the problem in private after class. Active listening does not give angry students a reason to fight you back; therefore, it may buy you a little time and spare a conflict in front of a class.

Anger: What is It? Anger is an emotion that results from our thinking. It can range from being a little irritated to furious rage. Our hormones and chemicals in the body are related. Anger can result from internal or external events. Many of us have been taught that anger is negative; therefore, we "stuff it" and do not know how to express it in a healthy manner. Many factors can contribute—socioeconomics, family issues, issues within the student, school/environmental issues. Often, anger results when we feel we have lost control over things that mean a great deal to us. Role-playing is an effective way to help students, parents and staff understand what anger is. In classrooms, faculty meetings, or PTA meetings, teachers can role-play situations that demonstrate anger

Anger Avenues: Ross Greene (2001) identifies what may be causes of angry, explosive behavior in children and young people.

- *A Difficult Temperament*—Some students may simply be born with the tendency to be difficult and such a temperament may not be a product of the environment. Dr. Greene suggests that these students may be characterized by a high activity level, may be easily distracted, may be loud and forceful, irregular in moods, physically sensitive, shy and reserved in new situations, and experience difficulty adapting to new situations.

- *ADHD*—Students with ADHD often have a low frustration tolerance which can lead to angry outbursts. What if you lived in a world where sounds, images, and thoughts were constantly moving? You felt helpless because you were not able to stay on tasks you needed to complete and you moved from one activity to another without any closure. You were so enclosed in this world that you often did not realize when someone spoke to you. These students are impulsive, inattentive, easily distracted, and don't follow through on tasks. The adults in their lives often view them as rebellious or non-compliant. When the students are doing well, these adults often feel the students should be able to control their own behavior. Relationships can de damaged, and students may experience low self-esteem and emotional pain. All of this can result in anger.

- *Social Skills Deficit*—Students with rigid thinking skills and the inability to be flexible can experience social problems that can lead to angry outbursts. These students have difficulty picking up their friends' social cues and lack the knowledge to respond appropriately. For instance, if one student slaps another on the back, the student with a social skills deficit may respond in anger because he cannot determine whether the slap was affectionate (Hey, buddy, how are you?) or really meant to be offensive.

- *Language Processing Problems*—Students who have problems expressing themselves verbally experience the frustration that can lead to explosive behavior.

- *Mood Disorders*—Students who are depressed may experience angry, explosive behavior. The depression must be treated before we can deal with the anger. Also, students need to be told of the depressant effects of drugs and alcohol since some angry behavior is the result of substance abuse.

- *Nonverbal Learning Disabilities*—Such students are often very concrete and attempt to negotiate a world that often isn't. They don't read cues well or respond to non-verbal communication. They may have difficulty finding their way around, coping with changes in routine and transitions, following instructions with several steps, asking many repetitive questions, becoming over-whelmed very easily, and being physically sensitive. These students may appear competent.

- *Sensory Integration Dysfunction*—Students with this problem are unable to successfully integrate touch, sight (such as bright lights), sound and movement. They may respond by being overly sensitive to one sense or under-responsive. Such a dysfunction can affect classroom performance. Such students may not be able to effectively organize themselves. They may under or over respond. They may avoid certain, clothes, textures. They may also be sensitive to loud noise. In younger children this condition may have motor skill side effects.

According to Dr. Greene, "…flexibility and frustration tolerance are not skills that come naturally to some children."

Additional Pathways to Anger:

- *Anxiety/ Fear*—Dr. Stanley Turecki (1985) described certain anxiety disorders that are based in fear for no apparent reason. Students may experience fatigue, worry, heart palpitations, dizziness, lack of sleep and gastrointestinal symptoms. Anxiety disorders may include phobias, panic disorder, post-traumatic stress disorder (PTSD) and obsessive–compulsive disorder. In generalized anxiety disorder, students worry often about everyday life and are anxious, edgy, irritable, and fatigues. Students with phobias have intense fear of an object or situation. In panic disorder, students may experience a racing heart, fainting, shortness of breath, and the feeling of choking or smothering. Students with Post Traumatic Stress Disorder feel terror caused by a traumatic event. They sometimes experience flashback. PDSD is possible result of any mental or physical trauma. Dr. Turecki also identified Negative Mood as an underlying cause of angry behavior. A student with a negative mood is often irritable and unable to visibly show pleasure.

ANGER DIARY

Date and Time _____

First Symptom(s) _____

_____

What triggered your anger response? _____

_____

Your response

Do you think you did well or not so well?

_____

_____

What was something you did well in this situation?

_____

_____

Is there something you can do in the future to better manage your anger?

_____

_____

Anger Disorders: Kassinove (1995) summarized the various anger disorders from the DSM-IV that vary in terms of length of the disorder and the symptoms. A trained psychologist or physician can assist a school to diagnose such a disorder.

• *Adjustment Disorder With Angry Mood*

Characteristics would be a predominant manifestation of anger, such as periods of angry affect and irritability, sullenness, anger outbursts, or behavioral displays not sufficient to fit conduct problems, such as irritable complaining and pickiness, snappiness, making but not acting on verbal or physical threats, slamming objects, or throwing things. According to DSM-IV, adjustment disorders are maladaptive reactions to identifiable psychosocial stressors that occur within three months after onset of the stressor, and have persisted for no longer than 6 months. An example would be a child or adolescent that is sullen, argumentative, irritable, and angry with his parents for moving away from established friends, school, and neighborhood.

- ### *Situational Anger Disorder Without Aggression*

This anger disorder describes a persistent (present 6 months or more), consistent and intense anger reaction to a circumscribed situation. Although the individual becomes demonstrably angry, he/she does not show significant aggressive behavior. An example would be a sixth grader who gets very angry when students crowd ahead of him/her in the lunch line. He/she may tense-up, get flushed in the face, curse internally, or complain to others. He/she will not be aggressive.

- ### *Situational Anger Disorder With Aggression*

This disorder involves both elevated anger and aggressive behavior in response to specific situations. An example would be Lewis, a fifth grader, who is usually an easy-going person until he is put in an uncomfortable or irritable situation. During a pick-up game of basketball he gets fouled, preventing him from scoring. He gets angry and yells and starts hitting the other player.

- ### *General Anger Disorder Without Aggression*

Whereas the situational anger disorders are circumscribed, this disorder describes the individual who is chronically and pervasively angry, but not highly aggressive. He/she always seems unhappy and/or irritable. The individual may occasionally behave aggressively, either verbally or against objects (e.g., make sharp comments, pout or sulk, slam doors).

- ### *General Anger Disorder With Aggression*

This disorder involves both frequent periods of generalized anger and frequent aggressive behavior. This disorder describes an individual who is frequently in an angry mood, but also does things such as engage in sarcasm, put others down, make verbal threats, or elevate discussions to loud arguments and yelling matches. For another individual, the mode of anger expression may be more physical than verbal.

Alleviate Stress by trying one of the following activities:

- Run

- Walk

- Talk to friends

- Lift weights

- Join a sports team

- Play sports with friends.

- Watch a movie

- Talk to someone you trust

- Take a stretching or yoga class

Anger Mapping: Try making a map like the one below. Write the problem in the space in the middle of the map, and write possible solutions to the problems on the lines around the center. Consider all your alternatives, and then choose the best one.

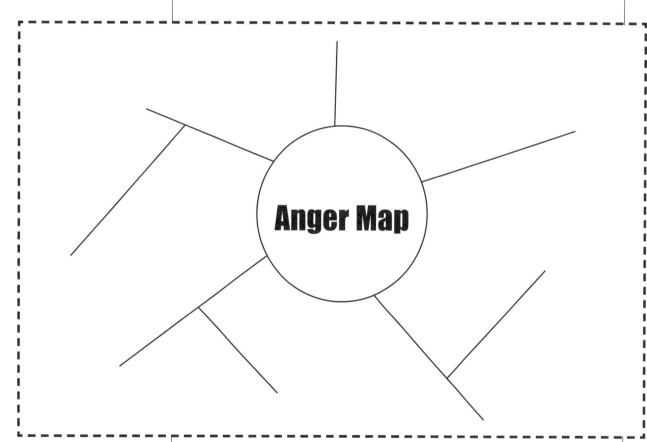

Adapted from a workshop handout by Tian Dayton, Ph.D. from
the Many Faces of Anger Conference, Nashville, Tenn. In May 1999.

Agree With It: If someone is teasing you, simply agree with them. For example, if someone says to you, "Your feet are too big," how about responding by saying, "You're right, they are pretty big. I'll let you know if they get any bigger."

Allies are Better than Enemies! Find a friend who will remind you of your plan to stay out of trouble. Give him/her permission to ask you to walk away from potentially dangerous situations. Remind him/her to talk you through the situation by reminding you of your plan and/or of the consequences.

Apologize: Teach students the importance of saying I'm sorry when doing something wrong. Although it doesn't take away the negative behavior, it goes a long way in mending a difficult situation. Students need to see this behavior modeled by the adults in their lives.

Assertive Behavior: Aggressive behavior means that you yell or talk down to someone else. Passive behavior means that you allow other people to yell or talk down to you. Assertive behavior simply means you talk neutrally to the other person without yelling or getting yelled out. This is the preferred behavior.

- Help students practice saying what they're feeling by using "I" statements.

- Teach students that being in a win-win situation means listening as well as talking.

- Set up a few role-plays to teach this. Show the difference in the styles of behavior, and talk about the consequences of each style.

Art: Young children are often unable to articulate the unresolved grief and loss that may lead to their anger. Children's art can be an effective way to begin such a conversation with children.

- Ask the child to draw a picture of a boy or girl his or her age.

- Look for eye detail—the lashes, the eyeball

- Unusual emphasis on the nostrils may indicate internal hostility.

- Teeth may appear sharper with blood dripping.

- Such art may indicate that a child is stuck in the grieving phase of anger

- Potter's clay is effective as well as sand trays to help students begin to talk about their grief. This strategy also works well with adolescents.

Ask the Students! Fenwick English in his book *What They Don't Tell You in Schools of Education about School Administration* said, "You can BS a BSer but you can't BS the kids." Student voice in schools is often an untapped resource. The perceptions of students are often more accurate than adult perceptions and can give us valuable information if we listen. Willert (2002) conducted a series of focus groups with high school students concerning the issue of school safety. Some of the students' thinking follows:

- Adults should hold students responsible for safety in their schools.

- Though safety was important, students in the study felt that stress was a larger issue- grades, college acceptance, and peer pressure.

- Students indicated that bullying and fighting occur frequently.

- Students were bored in most classes

- Students found many teachers "weak and uninspired" (p. 11) as well as lacking in caring about students beyond the classroom.

- They indicated that schools do not educate them about violence prevention and do not deal with students' feeling left out or being teased, bullied or assaulted.

Willert also recommends school climate analysis, staff development for teachers centered on student concerns, and counseling and intervention for bullying, teasing, and fighting.

Awareness Enhancement: If we become aware of something, we are then able to do something about it. We can...

- Interview and explore a student's anger history to find patterns.

- Encourage the student to make notes to him/herself when angry.

- Have the student imagine and recall an angry situation.

- Role-play and set up the interaction.

- Video the angry student and debrief the video with the student (with previous permission).

- Use questionnaires to stimulate discussion.

- The goal is to take the student off "automatic pilot" with his/her anger and move forward by seeking to disconnect the "triggers" to avoid the sequence leading to anger because the cues are removed.

Example: A student may need ten minutes to herself when she gets home before she interacts with the family.

Back-Up Systems: It's really important when dealing with angry students to have a back up system in place in case your first plan of attack doesn't work. Consider some of the following back up systems to use:

- Have a responsible student to get the principal in case of emergency. Discuss the plan with the student ahead of time.

- Have a buddy teacher. Assign a responsible student to lead the class to this teacher's room in case of problems.

- Have the principal observe your classroom if you believe there will be a problem.

- Have a pre-assigned place for angry students to go for time out.

- Have a place in your room where a student can put on earphones, listen to soothing music, relax, and chill out.

- Have a conference with the parents. Have the parents on stand-by in case you need them.

Reprinted with permission. Carr, Tom. (2000) 131 Creative Strategies
for Reaching Children with Anger Problems. Youthlight, Inc. Chapin, S.C.

Basic Needs: William Glasser (1998) stated that everyone has four basic psychological needs. It is very important try to meet these needs in appropriate ways or inappropriate behavior such as angry outbursts may result.

Psychological Need	Appropriate Ways to Meet This Need	Inappropriate Ways to Meet This Need
Love/Belonging	Family, friends, teachers, church, boy/girl scouts, 4H	• Gangs • Cults • Dangerous friends
Freedom	Making appropriate choices about school, home, and friends	• Fighting because you think someone is telling you what to do • Refusing to do work because you want to "show them"
Power	Playing on the football team, doing well in school, excelling in karate, demonstrating artistic or musical talent	• Bullying • Teasing • Rolling your eyes • Talking back • Intimidating others
Fun	Playing with friends and family, going to the movies, going out to eat, playing games, playing sports, participating in clubs, participating in church or service activities	• Gangs • Drugs • Alcohol • Weapons • Skipping school • Tobacco

Beware: Sometimes students will engage in a form of manipulation called triangulation. It works like this. Knowing an assistant principal may be preparing to take disciplinary action, a student may run to the counselor to "head off" the punishment. Educators can prevent this by staying in contact with each other and working together rather than being set up in conflict with each other by students.

Black, White Thinking: For the angry student, life is either win or lose, love or hate with no shades of gray. If there is evidence that it is not positive, then it must be negative. The reality is that the world is mostly indifferent or somewhere in the gray. Our job is to help the student to become a discriminate thinker.

Blaming: Blaming doesn't usually work. It's a way to try to shift the blame and not take responsibility. Offer students incentives for being honest and truthful about things they've done wrong. For example, if he/she is dishonest about this behavior problem, the consequence would be the loss of recess and "silent" lunch. If he/she is honest about this, there would only be one consequence.

Body Language: Watch your body language in situations involving conflict and remember some of the following suggestions:

- Maintain a good distance between you and the angry student.

- Do not approach a student at a fast pace—it feels too much like an invasion of private space and can be threatening to an angry person.

- Take a step back from the student to show that you are not a threat to the student.

- Talk very softly.

- Speak respectfully.

- Do not place any demands on the student.

Boundaries: Help adolescents create and enforce boundaries. "Who will touch my body? No, I will not do that!"

Boys—Tips for Parents: Dedman (2000) summarized Pollack's tips on listening to boys. An assistant professor of psychology at Harvard Medical School, Pollack was also the consultant to the Secret Service on the school shooters study.

- Allow the boy to choose the time to talk.

- Find a safe place for this talk, a place free of shame.

- Most boys like "action talk," connected to play or an activity.

- Do not tease or shame.

- Do not lecture; speak briefly and then wait,

- Speak from your own experience if it is relevant. This helps the boy know he is not alone.

- Listen quietly and very attentively.

- Let the boy know how much you love and care for him.

- Be certain that boys have regular undivided attention and "listening space."

- Don't expect independence if the boy is not ready.

- Support the boy in expressing a wide range of emotions and feelings.

- Explain that real men do cry and share their feelings.

- Express your love openly.

- When a boy engages in aggressive or angry behavior, look for the pain underneath.

Bullying: Bullying has been identified by the Secret Service as a significant factor in school shootings with the shooters taking the role of victim. The issue has also come to the attention of medical professionals as evidenced in the April 25, 2002 issue of *The Journal of the American Medical Association.* In this article, Pace defines bullying as an imbalance of power, an intention to harm or disturb. It involves repeated occurrences, psychological and emotional. It occurs in both genders, all races and ethnicities, and all socio-economic levels. Bullying can be verbal, such as name-calling and threats, or physical, such as pushing or hitting.

Bullying Signs: Victims of bullying can be recognized by the following signs:

- Avoiding certain situations, people, or places.

- Truancy, changes in behavior, being withdrawn, passive, overly active and aggressive or self-destructive.

- Frequent crying, feeling sad, signs of low self-esteem, unwilling to speak

- Showing signs of fear when asked about certain situations, people, and places.

- Signs of injuries, recurrent unexplained physical symptoms (stomach pains, fatigue)

- Suddenly receiving lower grades or showing signs of learning problems.

Bullying Research: Pace in the April 25, 2002 issue of *The Journal of the American Medical Association,* indicates that the initial research on bullying was conducted mostly in Europe and reported that school based bullying interventions resulted in up to 50% reductions in reported bullying. These interventions included:

- Curricular on social skills

- Clear rules and consequences

- Increased supervision from and the presence of parents,

- Services for those bullying and those being bullied.

Bullying Tips: Frankel (1996) makes the following suggestions:
- Focus on the victim rather than the bully immediately following the incident.

- Get as much detail as possible from the victim.

- Take charge. Doing nothing condones it.

- Increase the victim's self-esteem.

- Warn the victim to refuse to follow through with any dangerous demands but seek protection from the nearest adult.

- Protect the victim from the bully

- Notify the bully's parents

- Have the bully write a letter of apology to the student; an oral one could be sarcastic

- Have a consequence if the bully goes within 20 feet of the victim.

- Handle the problem in class meetings so that peers rather than adults confront the bully.

- Provide service or altruistic opportunities for the bully.

- Make sure the bully receives counseling

Bullying Victims
- Get the details from the student allowing him or her to express feelings.

- Rehearse with the student how to make fun of the teasing… "So what? And your point is?"

- Ask if the student used the technique and how it worked.

- Pair up the student with a peer mentor or another caring adult.

Bully Fighters

- Intervene with the fighter according to school policy.

- Get all the details from the student.

- Teach the victim to avoid the fighter
    - Don't talk to him or her.
    - Protect yourself by staying out of the bully's reach
    - Play close to the yard monitor or hang out at school in a supervised area.
    - Don't tease or make faces at the bully

- Follow up with the victim. Did these strategies work?

Bully Busters: Try a few of the following strategies to try to turn bullies into leaders.

- Give the bully a job.

- Ask the bully to protect a victim.

- Challenge the bully to complete a service project.

- Get several students who bully to work together to raise money to give to the homeless shelter or some other local service organization.

- Provide the bully with strategies to walk away from the problem.

- Ask the bully to take care of a class pet.

- Involve the bully in a peer listener program.

Bully Contracts: Carolina Day Middle School in Asheville, North Carolina used a survey and discussion with students to generate the bully behavior contract below.

Reprinted with the permission of Peggy Daniels, principal, Carolina Day Middle School.

Bullying Behaviors as Defined by the CDS Middle School Student Council and Included in the Middle School Student Handbook, p. 5

Bullying

At Carolina Day School, bullying is defined as behavior that is mean, unkind, or unpleasant to another. It is an intent to hurt or harm someone else, either physically, emotionally, or both.

The following examples of bullying-type behaviors were generated by CDS middle school student and further defined by the Middle School Student Council as examples of behaviors to avoid. Bullying includes but is not limited to the behaviors listed below.

Behaviors to Avoid

Physical Bullying
Pulling hair / pinching / tripping
Shoving / twisting arms / kicking
Punching / flicking / hitting
Pushing someone against a locker
Being overly aggressive in P.E. or intramurals
Blocking another person's way
Glaring / Staring
Bumping into other people
Taking / Hiding / Damaging someone's property
Touching people in inappropriate ways
Getting into another's space

Exclusion
Saving seats
Not giving others a chance to be involved
Singling people out because of differences
Telling secrets
Talking behind people's backs
Leaving a small number of people out
    when planning or hosting a social event
    (i.e. inviting 10 of 12 girls in your class to a sleep-over)

Making Fun / Teasing / Taunting
Laughing at someone
Playing pranks / Pestering / Mimicking
Using "just kidding" as a
    response to hurtful teasing
Making negative remarks about the
    characteristics, abilities, or skills
    of another

Other Types of Bullying
Put downs / Insults / Sneering
Calling someone "stupid" / Cussing
Derogatory remarks / Finding fault
    with others
Starting or spreading rumors
Bossing someone around
Taking anger out on others
Annoying or irritating another repeatedly
Using words and actions to turn students
    against other students

My signature indicates that I have read and understand this information and that I am willing to make a commitment not to bully.

Name_____Date_____

Boosting Anger in Others: One of the greatest drives of all human beings is the drive to be in control. The healthy way to be in control is to be in control of you—autonomy. Some students seek control by controlling others. It is very powerful to stand back and watch others escalate due to your efforts. For adolescents there is the added confusion of the "pack mentality." Banding together against the victim can be rewarding on some levels and difficult to stop. Be sure to implement the following:

- Group rewards and group consequences

- One-on-one discussions with students to focus on their own positive goals

- Peer support for positive goals

- Peer input for discipline issues

Break the Cycle: Once an angry child gets going, he/she may sometimes be on his/her way to having a pretty bad day. If you see the anger building, help the child to break the cycle by doing something different. Try one of the following strategies:

- Write from 1-100.

- Draw a picture.

- Run laps around the playground.

- Run an errand for the teacher.

- Restack books in the back of the room.

- Listen to music with headphones.

- Put together a puzzle.

Catharsis: Rage can actually be fueled by catharsis. Bushman, Baumeister, and Stack (1999) conducted a study in which subjects were still angry after hitting a punching bag and then lashed out in a game. The researchers concluded that catharsis that involves hitting often fuels rage. Instead of teaching students to punch, squeezing something may be more appropriate. Alternatives to punching include art, clay, and sand tray therapy.

Challenge the Norms: The norms around a school campus are very well defined.

- Most students think it's "cool" to fight.

- Most think you are a chicken if you walk away from a fight.

- Most think that fighting is the way to be tough.

- Most think you're "not a man" if you don't fight.

- Most think that teasing and putting others down keeps you in the "cool group."

These beliefs are sad, but true in many schools. Challenge students to begin thinking about what they believe. Do their beliefs come from the media, from music, from their parents, or maybe even from their friends? What can your school do about this?

- Can you give a consequence for watching a fight?

- Can you get some of those "cool" kids to walk around and help kids who appear to be victimized?

- Can you try to raise awareness of what put down remarks are about?

The point is to just do something to challenge the norms to get kids thinking. Education may be the first step to change.

Children in Trouble: Price, et.al (2002) studied elementary children in an urban setting to assess their experience with carrying weapons, violence, concerns for personal safety and their perceptions concerning resolving fights. Of the 1912 fourth and fifth graders, one in 12 had carried a weapon one or more times in the past month. One third said they would hit their peers back if they were hit. One fourth did not feel safe going to and from school. Between 23 and 43 percent were concerned about being attacked in or around school. The authors suggest that waiting until middle school to teach anger management, conflict resolution, and problem-solving skills is too late.

Clear, Consistent Rules and Procedures: Students always watch the adults in their lives. They need school-wide rules clearly stated and consistently enforced. This is one of the signs of a healthy school climate. Faculties need to have conversations about the rules and their consistent enforcement.

Closed Fist: Try this activity!

- Pick a partner

- One person makes the tightest fist possible.

- The other does "whatever it takes" to get that person to open his or her fist.

- Debrief the different strategies used.

What does this tell us about dealing with someone who is angry or hostile?

Cognitive Strategies: Help the student see cognitive contrasts—"You were really angry at your teacher on Tuesday but just irritated on Thursday. What were you thinking those days?" The point is that how the student thinks about it makes a difference. The goal is to establish relevance for change. Ask questions like, "What if you thought about it this way?" What if you said, "Hey, I'm not getting through the intersection because traffic is so bad"? That happens some days'."

Comebacks: Practice using great comebacks to give students an unexpected response and to diffuse an angry situation. For example, if a student says:

- You are the meanest teacher I've ever had.
  Response: Thanks, I've been working really hard to get to this point.

- You are not fair.
  Response: You may be right.

- You are a real b-----!
  Response: Have you been talking to my husband?

- You make me sick!
  Response: I'm sorry. Do you need to go to the bathroom?

The point of the comebacks is to provide an unexpected response so that you can show students that their anger is not controlling you or pushing your buttons in any way.

Communication: Communication involves listening and talking. Do a few activities to discuss the importance of positive communication.

- Get a box of yellow sticky notes. Write positive and negative statements on each sticky note. Walk around the room and say what is written on each note. Stick these notes on other students. Tell students that our words are like this—they stick all over people. It's important what we say. People may remember our words for a lifetime.

- Play the labels game. Write a few positive and a few negative statements on labels. Divide the children into groups of four or five, and ask them to stick the labels on their foreheads. Ask them to complete a project while at the same time treating others the way their label indicates. For example, a label might read, "I'm smart, ask me lots of questions." or "I have a hard time learning; treat me like I'm stupid." Ask students how they felt when treated like their label. Ask them if communication has the power to make us angry or glad. Discuss.

- Play the gossip game. Tell one student a sentence and ask him/her to whisper it around in the circle. Of course it will get mixed up. Talk about how gossip gets mixed up and ends up hurting people's feelings.

- Play the compliment game. Ask everyone to write their name on a sheet of notebook paper and pass this around the room. Ask each student to write down one positive compliment on each person's sheet. Make sure to emphasize to students that anyone breaking this rule will be removed from the game. Negative comments should not be tolerated. As the papers are being passed, ask students to try to catch negative statements so you can deal with the problem before the paper is given to its owner.

Communicating with Open Questions and Feeling Responses:

These are good questions and responses to use in working with an angry student.

Open Questions:
❑ How do you handle your anger?

❑ What do you think you should do about the situation?

❑ What is important to you?

❏ What happened in your last period class?

❏ How can you change the situation?

❏ What are you not able to control?

Feeling Responses:
❏ You're afraid you will lose your best friend.

❏ You're confused about what to do.

❏ You are very concerned about your reputation.

❏ You are frustrated with your math teacher.

❏ You feel treated unfairly.

❏ You're angry with your best friend.

Conflict Resolution: Research by Breunlin & Cimmarusti, et.al (2002) showed positive results for a conflict resolution skills training program in a large public high school of over 3000 near Chicago and focused on students who had been suspended for physical violence (fighting). The program was offered as an alternative to out-of-school-suspension. The results?

• There was a statistically significant difference between the groups who received that training and those who did not. Those who went through the program received no expulsions.

• All students who completed the program were four times less likely to receive another out of school suspension for fighting.

Confronting an Angry Student:
Berry (1994) suggested that adults confronting the aggressive students need to be aware of their own verbal and nonverbal behaviors. He recommended the following steps.

• Remain calm, in control

• Listen and use an empathetic assertion. Do not judge. " I realize you are upset and I understand."

• Be cognizant of your tone, volume and rate of speech. Use a calm tone, a moderate volume, and speak clearly and slowly.

• Use the student's name.

- Give choices and consequences and set limits. "If you go back to your seat, we can continue with class. If not, we will need to go to the principal's office."

Berry observed that much more of our communication is nonverbal than verbal. This is very important to consider in dealing with an agitated student.

- Respect 2 to 3 feet of the student's personal space and keep at least one leg length away.

- Turn your body from the student at a slight angle with hands in plain view and open. Never point your finger and do not cross your arms so as not to appear threatening.

- Make eye contact without staring. Eye contact is an issue in some cultures. Appear serious but not angry or afraid.

- Do not stand over the student. This is threatening and demeaning.

In Case of Attack

Schools should identify and train teams who are located in various locations of the school. These individuals should be divided into three person teams to respond to aggressive students. All teachers and staff members should be able to call for help through effective communications systems. The first person on the scene takes charge, assesses the situation and communicates with the student. The other two members remove the gathering crowd from the scene and then assist with the safe removal and transportation of the aggressive student from the scene to a more private location.

If help does not arrive immediately and you are attacked, Berry suggests you protect yourself with the least force necessary and try to keep the student from being hurt. Increase your personal space quickly. Dodge blows if you can. If the student grabs you, twist away. When other adults arrive, safely restrain the student if he or she is still being aggressive. Much will depend on the nature of the situation. Training in restraint techniques is recommended.

Creative Incentives: Use creative incentives to motivate children to do their best. When a student had made progress in controlling anger behaviors, these ideas might be useful:

- Dominoes—Upon exhibiting positive behaviors, give students a chance to choose a domino and add up the dots to determine how many points he/she receives. After a certain amount of time, students may turn in the points for a prize or save up the points for a better prize.

- Classroom creatures—Provide students with the opportunity to take care of a rabbit, gerbil, bird, or other creature.

- Balloon prizes—Write the names of various prizes on slips of paper and place them inside balloons. Blow up the balloons. Give children a choice of popping a balloon to retrieve a prize.

- Phone home when a student does well.

Cognitive Restructuring: Challenge students to restructure their belief systems if their beliefs are causing them problems. For example,

Activating Event	Belief about the event	Consequence
Susan teases me.	No one likes me. Everyone thinks I'm terrible. She'll tell everyone about this. I can't stand this anymore.	Crying Sulking Not wanting to come to school Fearful Sad
Susan teases me.	I'll just tell her to leave me alone. It's not true anyway, so why should I care? All of my real friends know how she is. They won't pay her any attention, so why should I?	Annoyed, but nothing extreme Detached from the problem No crying No sulking Better attitude

Catch Yourself before you say the wrong thing. Try to learn to think before you speak. Realize that you can't take it back if you ever say it. Make yourself a back-up plan. Walk away before you say the wrong thing to keep yourself out of trouble.

Centering: Teach centering techniques (finding a quiet place, relaxing, thinking positive thoughts).

Choices: Choices are very important with everyone but especially with angry students. Make sure you don't back these students "against the wall". When students are threatened with no way out but to fight, they will usually choose to do just that. Be sure to phrase most everything as a choice. For example,

- Would you like to walk to the principal's office alone or with another teacher?

- Would you like to do the even or the odd problems?

- Would you like to stay inside during recess or sit on the bench?

Chronically Angry Students: Fryxell (2000) studied fifth and sixth graders and generated risk factors to identify chronically angry students:

- Pre-adolescent youth without sufficient material and mental support at home (divorced, separated, single parent families)

- Pre-adolescent youth who do poorly in school.

- Students identified by teachers as struggling with making and keeping friends, who are teased, or have poor social skills.

- Pre-adolescent youth with poor self esteem.

- Students in this study were found to be capable of understanding their difficulties with anger. Therefore students who self-select should be in this group.

Develop a Relationship: This is one of the best tools for working with angry students. They need someone to trust and someone to talk to. If they trust you, you'll have a better chance of talking them down from a difficult situation. If you've ever looked around, there's usually someone who can even talk to the most difficult student. Remember those basic needs. Everyone needs to feel loved and important.

Detach Yourself from the Problem: If a student is yelling at you or angry with you for some reason, try to keep yourself detached by trying some of the following strategies:

- Pretend the student is calling you something ridiculous. For example, pretend that the student just called you a can of Tuna.

- Repeat your to-do list silently in your mind. Going to the dry cleaners, cooking dinner, picking up a gallon of milk, are usually pretty boring things. Hopefully, this will get your mind off of the situation in front of you.

- Tell the student that you cannot talk to him/her while he/she is angry. Remove yourself from the situation if possible. Get the student to time-out.

Debrief: Debrief students who have an angry outburst by waiting until the outburst is entirely over and the student is totally calmed down. Allow the student to tell you what happened. Deal with the consequences. Make amends if necessary and try to help the student make a better plan for next time. Never try to complete this procedure in the middle of an outburst. The student will always need time to cool off.

Denial: Often angry students are in denial about their problems. Sometimes the underlying problem is unresolved grief, sometimes a symptom of drug/alcohol abuse, and sometimes a divorce of their parents. The anger is coming from somewhere, but students sometimes don't want to deal with the real problem. Develop a relationship with the student so that you can hopefully help them to begin dealing with the real issues.

Diamonds and Stones: Goleman's (1995) work on emotional intelligence reveals that one quality of emotionally intelligent individuals is the ability to self-disclose. Often students who are new to a school or who are unable to verbalize their feelings to another person may benefit from this activity on safe self-disclosure.

- Give each group or classroom member an index card.

- Instruct students not to write their names on the card and to disguise their handwriting. Instruct them not to use the names of any other individuals in the activity

- On one side of the card, the students should write the word Diamonds and on the other side the word Stones.

- Under Diamonds, students should list the things in their lives that are going well.

- On the other side under Stones, students should list the things that are not going so well.

- The adult leading the exercise should complete a card also.

- The adult should collect all the cards, shuffle them, and redistribute them to the students and keep a card. Students should be told that if they should get their own card, they should return it to the adults who will give them another card.

- The adult then models and "becomes" the person on the card by saying, "These are the diamonds in my life," and describing what is on the card. Then do the same with the stones.

- The students then do the same. The activity is more effective if the student stands.

- When all cards have been described, the adult should ask the students if they noticed common patterns in the diamonds as well as the stones.

One of the values of this activity besides encouraging safe self-disclosure is that when students hear that others in the group or class experience many of their same problems, they realize they are not alone. New students in the school benefit especially.

Distracters: Some chronically anger-prone students need to be kept busy and distracted. They may not do well with time on their hands. They may require help in getting off the anger track and on the learning track.

- ***The Bag of Surprises…*** Keep on hand a "surprise bag" to pull out when things are going downhill. For younger students this may literally be a bag, box, or other type of "hidden surprise box". You may choose to stop class, with an air of excitement, and allow a student to reach, blindly, into the container, and try to identify the object. Or, you may reach in, offer a few hints, and see who can guess the contents. For older students the surprise would need to be more sophisticated.

- *Name that Tune…* Popular music CDs may be pulled out for a "name that tune" moment. Or, an audio game with pre-recorded sounds captured from the environment for a "guess the sound" game. You could prepare for this activity by sending a team of "recording engineers" around the school to make the recording. The tape could be kept on hand for a time when you need this distracter.

- *The Crafty Break…* Have on hand a box of craft supplies for a "working break". This may be as simple as drawing paper and crayons, or as complicated as pre-cut birdhouse kits. (A state youth prison had juveniles participate in making birdhouses and giving them to nursing home residents. This activity helped to build skills, decrease fighting, and allow the juveniles to give back to the community.)

- *Drop Everything And Read!* This surprise consists of an engaging book that you are reading to the class. You may choose to pull the book out for moments of needed escape. It is especially engaging if you are able to present the book with dramatic voices and gestures. Move about the room as you read, drawing the students into the story with your enthusiasm and energy.

A footnote: If you use these distracters for mental escape, or to respond to a growing problem, it will become apparent to your students what you are doing. There is nothing wrong with this! In fact, it should be a lesson to all that one way to manage a difficult moment is to take a bit of a timeout.

Drug/Alcohol Abuse: Certain substances can put kids on edge and cause them to act out at the slightest provocation. Be aware of this and talk to parents about it. Although you can't make an accusation to parents, you can describe their child's behavior and ask them what they think it could be. Some parents may deny any problems; some may get the child treatment.

Do Something Out of the Ordinary: When students are trying to get the best of you by saying or doing something they believe will make you angry, do something out of the ordinary. For example, if you are writing on the board and the students all drop their books at one time, you might turn around look at your watch, drop your book, say "Sorry, I was a little late", and keep on teaching.

Desensitization: Ask the students to think about themselves in certain situations that make them fearful. Ask them to DRAW a PIC-TURE of themselves dealing with the situation in a positive manner. Ask them to imagine themselves in this difficult situation behaving in a strong manner. Hopefully these thoughts will help the students gain confidence for dealing with difficult situations.

Don't Bug Me Chair: Place a special chair in your room where students can sit if they are having a bad day. When in this chair, make a rule that other students cannot bother or talk to this person.

Door to Door Diffusion: If a student comes in angry, try to diffuse the situation before it gets really bad by trying this strategy. Make an arrangement with several of your colleagues by explaining the following procedures. Place a certain color of dot on a note asking these teachers for a certain item. The dot is the signal to the teacher that this is an SOS call and consequently that he/she should not actually have the item that the note is asking for. It also signals the teacher to spend a little time complimenting the student. The teacher may tell the angry child that he/she has heard something particularly nice about him/her or that the child looks particularly nice on this day. The purpose of the plan is for the student to actually see about three people who are positive and complimentary and therefore hopefully get him/her on a better track for the day.

Don'ts

Remember the "don'ts" when being teased or bullied by others.

- Don't let them see you cry. Some bullies like this and will keep teasing you if you cry.

- Don't let them see you acting fearful. Bullies know they've gotten the best of you.

- Don't walk into a dangerous situation. Be smart. Walk around, get some friends to walk with you, etc.

- Don't tease the person back. This puts you in a situation that could make things worse.

- Don't antagonize a bully. It will only make things worse.

• Don't participate in dangerous activities like jokes that hurt others, drug/alcohol abuse, gossip, etc. These things only hurt others.

Do's

Remember the do's of dealing with bullies.

• Do think of a plan like telling the person you don't like what he or she is doing.

• Do walk away from a dangerous situation if necessary.

• Do ignore some things if possible.

• Do get an adult to help if necessary.

• Do show a strong face and a strong attitude even if you feel weak on the inside.

• Do stand tall when dealing with bullies.

• Do find something positive about the bully and try to focus on that.

Escape Passes: Offer students several escape passes. Determine a pre-established place that a student can go if he/she is feeling a little anxious or angry. This place might be the water fountain, a "buddy teacher", a counselor, etc. Hopefully, this will help the student learn to recognize how he/she is feeling before a blow-up and learn to redirect his/her attention to calm down and regain control.

Reprinted with permission. Carr, Tom. (2000)131 Creative Strategies for Reaching Children with Anger Problems. Youthlight, Inc. Chapin, S.C.

Eliminate Potential Frustrations: Some situations may trigger anxiety or anger in children. Be on the lookout for these situations and simply remove them if possible. This might be an unstructured time in the classroom, a music class where it is very loud, or free play at recess. Every child is different. If restructuring their day is an option, simply make a few changes until the child has learned more effective coping skills.

Empathy: Help students to learn empathy so that they can recognize how others feel as a result of behaviors such as bullying, teasing, etc. Try the following activities:

• Ask students to draw a picture of a flower with five petals. Ask them to write or draw the following things on each of the petals:

1—The name of someone you were close to but now lost

2—The name of someone who believes you are special

3—Something you would like to do when you grow up

4—The name of one of your best friends

5—Something special that you remember from when you were younger

After completing this flower, ask students to change papers with a partner. Ask the partner to then wad up the paper in a little ball. Children will be surprised because they think you would have asked them to share the information. After this, explain that you have made a mistake and you would like for them to try to straighten out the piece of paper and give it back to their partner.

Discussion: Explain that this is how friendships are. When we gossip about our friends or hurt their feelings, we damage the relationship a little bit. Sure it can be straightened out with an apology, but it just doesn't ever look the same. Discuss the importance of being careful with your friend's feelings when they entrust them to you.

Enforceable Words: Fay and Funk (1995) offer this activity. Try to use statements that you really can enforce with students. For example if you say to an angry student, "You're going to sit here until you finish this work," can you really enforce this? Does this mean that you'll spend the night until the work is finished? Of course it doesn't and students know that. Only use enforceable statements that encourage appropriate choices on the student's part. For example, another way to say that might be: "Feel free to go outside when you've finished your work." This sounds better and is certainly less confrontational.

Evacuation Plans: Evacuation is the act of removing, departing from, withdrawing, or vacating, especially from a threatened area. Students who are escalating with anger often need to have a brief "vacation" from the present situation. We sometimes refer to this as timeout. Ideally, it is used as a preventive measure, to prevent things from getting worse, and to allow a cool-down time.

❏ *I'll Meet You Outside…* Calmly state to the student that you will meet her outside the classroom, then walk to the area. Expect the student to follow you. It is important to handle this calmly, privately, and quietly.

❏ *Please Run this Errand for Me…* Ask the student to take a message to the room down the hall, or to the office. Give the student time to get away from the classroom. Go outside the room to meet the student and have a one-to-one discussion.

❏ *Hold a "Side-bar"…* Ask the student to meet you in another area of the room. Again, this is a quiet request. The intent is to break the momentum of escalating anger by walking to another area, then to have a brief talk.

❏ *The "Buddy Bouncer"…* Identify a student that you can count on to accompany the angry student on an errand, or simply to take a walk.

❏ *"All Hands on Deck… Man the Lifeboats"…* There are rare occasions where the angry student is escalating and will not respond to any attempt to help them leave the area to calm down. In these situations, it may be necessary to ask all the other students to leave and go to another area. Of course, this requires at least one adult to be with both the group of students and with the individual angry student.

Fear: Alexander (2002) described a 2001 survey of 15,000 teenagers around the United States. These were the findings.

- More than one in three students felt unsafe in school.

- 43 percent of high school boys and 37 percent of middle school boys believe it is okay to hit or threaten anyone who has made them angry.

- 75 percent of boys and 60 percent of girls had hit someone in the past twelve months because they were angry.

- 21 percent of high school boys and 15 percent of middle school boys possessed a weapon on school grounds during the last year.

- 60 percent of high school boys and 31 percent of middle school boys said they could get a gun if they wanted to.

Find Out if there's a reason for the anger
- Is there abuse going on?

- Does the situation at hand remind you of something that has happened to you in the past?

- Do you know of something different you could do in this situation?

- Do you somehow enjoy the power that the anger gives you?

- Do you really feel scared or powerless inside?

If you can figure out the underlying problem, then you can begin to determine what to do about the outward problem of anger.

Fight Smarter: Being aggressive is not necessary in order to deal with a situation, but having a smart plan of action is. Many people often believe that being aggressive or being passive are the only ways of dealing with an issue. Being assertive is the best way – that way you take care of yourself and the other person in the process. Develop a plan where you are not the victim or the aggressor. This plan might include talking assertively to the person and telling them your feelings, or it might even include talking firmly to the person to tell them to leave you alone. Whatever the solution, the outcome is that you feel better for having dealt with the problem in a positive manner.

Forgiveness: Eventually, it is necessary to forgive yourself and to forgive other people. This takes time and is usually something you can't do right away. It's O.K. to feel angry about a problem and try to deal with the problem, but eventually continuing to hang on to anger becomes toxic. In fact, holding on to anger usually doesn't hurt the other person as much as it hurts you, and people can become unhappy and unhealthy when allowing anger to fester. Forgiveness means letting go of the problem; it does not mean condoning the action. Forgiving someone else means you let the anger go and consciously make a decision to quit expending your energy on the problem. Forgiving yourself means you learn from your mistakes and even feel badly about what you've done, but eventually let it go and quit spending too much time and energy beating yourself up.

Football Field: Draw a football field on the board and draw a figure representing the class. Tell the class that their goal is to make a touchdown. Once they make the touchdown, they will receive some pre-arranged reward. For example, the class might receive an extra play period, a movie (perhaps about a piece of literature you're studying), a popcorn party, etc. Pre-establish the rules of the game. Every time the class does what you ask of them in a set time period, move the figure a certain amount of yards down the field. Penalties will be called when the class does not do what you ask of them in the set amount of time. Consequently, the figure is moved back on the field. The goal of this activity is to encourage students to work together as a team.

Give Students The Last Word: Sometimes students just want to have the last word. Go ahead and tell them that he/she can have the last word. That way, you're still in control of the conversation and the student perceives he/she has received what he/she wanted. Say, "I am giving you permission to have the last word."

Give the Student a Chance for Success: In order to do this, try to remember the following suggestions:
- Speak privately to a student. Try to never embarrass a child in front of the class.

- Make sure to remove the "audience." If other students are watching, the angry student may not choose to back down.

- Do not lose your temper. It will only make the student more angry.

- Do not be confrontational. Anger plus anger equals trouble.

- Do not touch an angry student.

Games: Games are a great way to practice using conflict resolution and anger management strategies. Games are a wonderful way to reinforce these strategies.

- Games often offer quickly timed responses from students so that students have to learn to think "on their feet."

- Students need repetition to over-learn the concepts so that the ideas come naturally in emotionally-charged situations.

- Games are non-threatening.

- Games are fun.

Girls—Tips for Parents: While boys often express their anger physically, girls more often use gossip, rumors, and name-calling. Rosalind Wiseman (2001) in her popular book *Queen Bees and Wannabes* uses anecdotal evidence to make the following suggestions to parents of girls:

- Accept the possibility that your daughter can be a bully. Silence only reinforces the behavior.

- Support and believe your daughter when she says she is a victim of a bully.

- Intervene appropriately if your daughter is a victim or a bully. Resist the temptation to go first to the other parents. Girls after the age of ten need to learn to negotiate conflicts.

- Do not model gossiping about other girls to your daughter. She is listening.

- Don't live your own life through your daughter. She is unique and her own special person.

- Know that you will not always like everything your child does. Life is like that.

- Remember to be a role model. This is a powerful position.

- Find opportunities to discuss sex with your daughter.

- Make a special effort to praise your daughter's accomplishments and not just her physical appearance.

- Help your daughter find exercise or activities to manage stress or channel her creativity. Girls enjoy writing and art. They also love causes, such as animal rights.

Grief and Loss: Much anger comes from grief and loss. Many students are grieving over the loss of a parent, a best friend, a grandparent, or even a pet. Some students can seemingly get through a situation pretty well, while others seem to have extreme reactions to similar situations. Resulting problems might include greater tendencies towards depression, feelings of low self-worth, feelings of being lost and out of control, general anger towards other people, possible thoughts of suicide, and decreased performance at school. It is important to get professional treatment if you know that a student is having a hard time dealing with grief and loss.

Robert Bowman, Ph.D. (2001) estimated that roughly 85 percent of internally hostile students have unresolved issues of grief and loss. These children, he feels, are stuck in the anger stage of grieving. He argues that we must work on these grief and loss issues in addition to dealing with the anger-related behavior. Deep chronic anger may manifest itself in aggression or even over-pleasing. Students may internalize their anger resulting in asthma, ulcers, and eating disorders. These students need an emotionally significant person to do lots of listening. In addition to anger groups in school and other settings, professionals should also consider grief and loss groups.

Good Behavior Book: Keep a book describing really nice things you've done for other people. This might include things as simple as times you've complimented others, times when you've helped others with homework, times you've made friends with students who didn't have friends, or times you've helped your parents at home. The most important thing especially for the student who constantly gets in trouble is to begin developing positive self-esteem by reaching out to other people.

Gossiping: Gossiping is a way to really get people angry. Many fights and arguments seem to erupt over what someone has said about someone else. Use a few activities to talk about gossiping and also to teach the art of complimenting others.

- First, challenge students to fill up a piece of paper with toothpaste. Then challenge them to put the toothpaste back in the tube. Explain that our words are like toothpaste; once it comes out, it can't go back in.

- Play the old gossip game by spreading a sentence around the circle. After it reaches the end, show how different it has become from the initial sentence. Play the game several times and encourage students to try to get it right. Show that even when trying to pass along accurate information, it often gets mixed up.

- Place a piece of paper on someone's back. Ask students to walk around the room and write compliments on each other's papers (i.e. Talking behind someone's back). Read the statements to each other.

- Pass around a piece of paper or paper plate with the name of the person written at the top. Ask students to write positive statements about the person as the paper is passed. (Make sure that students do not write negative statements by making it clear at the beginning of the activity that students will be unable to participate upon breaking this rule.)

Group of Angry Students: In working with a group of angry students, follow these guidelines.

- Establish clear and reasonable ways of conducting class… Students need and will demand order, predictability, and consistency. While they may complain about "silly rules", in their absence they almost seem to be forcing the creation of rules by acting out, perhaps seeking to create their own order. When establishing classroom rules, consider student input and a focus on logical expectations to accomplish the reason for the class (learning and playing together). Always remember that students want an emotionally and physically safe environment.

- Meet individually with students on a regular basis…One-on-one, students are a different breed. While it is sometimes inconvenient to meet with them individually, doing so can allow you to "divide and influence (versus conquer)" a group of students that tends to band together.

- In your plans, focus on positive goals for the students…Let's go out on a limb about this: ALL students start school with a desire to be successful, to learn, to do the right thing. Somewhere along the way they may get confused, but the teacher is always on sounder ground when focusing on the positive goals for students. It should be clear that rules and staff behaviors are not designed for the convenience or comfort of staff, but are for the positive benefit of students. For example, when trying to keep the school bathrooms clean, instead of saying, "If you don't keep this place clean, you won't be able to have paper in the bathroom", say, "You deserve to have a clean bathroom…" This focus on the benefit of students catches their attention.

- Be calm and deliberate regarding consequences. Follow through. Mean what you say.

- Seek peer support for positive goals. Faculty should be consistent and "singing off of the same page."

Humor: Try using humor to diffuse a difficult situation. If someone is teasing you, say something that is funny or tell a joke of some kind. For example:

- *Your house is ugly.*
  Response: That's because we hired ugly painters to paint it.

- *You are so stupid.*
  Response: Thanks! I subscribe to Stupid Weekly to get new ideas.

Healthy is In! Anger is not good for the health. Some people try unhealthy things to deal with anger. Some of these things might include smoking, drinking, taking drugs, over-eating, yelling, throwing fits, etc. None of these are good for the body. Instead of doing those things, try some of the following:

- Talking to friends about the problem

- Making a plan to deal directly with the problem in an assertive way

- Running

- Walking

- Going to a movie

- Writing in a journal

- Drawing pictures

- Getting away from the problem that is bothering you

In other words:

- Don't let the anger control you.

- Don't let the anger fester inside.

- Don't dwell on the anger constantly.

- Don't store up anger until you explode.

Hot Topics: Have classroom meetings to discuss things that make students "hot" or very angry. You may want to discuss teasing, bullying, gossiping, etc. Ask the class to brainstorm what you might do about this. Choose some of the best ideas, take a class vote, and implement the plan. *(See the B's section for bullying.)*

Help: Some students are angry and really need help. Make sure counselors, teachers, social workers, principals, etc. all let students and parents know that they are all on the same team ready to help provide better solutions for tough problems. Victims and bullies alike need help finding better solutions.

Hate Language: Ask students to list various types of language that may imply hateful or inappropriate comments. Certain comments like the ones listed below are inappropriate. Some students may say that he/she is "just kidding". Explain that these statements are not funny and should never be said to anyone for any reason. Discuss the implications and consequences of such statements

- I'll kill her.

- People like that don't deserve to live.

- I'll just beat him up.

- I'll just smash his face in.

- I don't like anyone who is (religious, ethnic, socioeconomic background.) They should be shot.

- I'll get my daddy's gun and bring it to school.

I messages: Use *I messages* when talking with people. *I messages* are non-blaming and help diffuse any volatile situations. It is important to teach students how to use these messages when confronting others about difficult behaviors.

Intrinsic Motivation: Although extrinsic motivation is helpful and sometimes beneficial in correcting negative behavior, intrinsic motivation is much more powerful in changing behaviors in the long run. Developing relationships with difficult students goes a long way for many reasons:

• Students need to feel trusted and respected in order to begin to make an attempt toward being compliant with you.

• Students need a safe and trusted person with whom they can open up and share problems about serious situations.

• The positive aspects of the relationship go a long way in helping calm a student down or getting him/her to quit doing a particular behavior.

Journal Conversation: Think of a person with whom you are currently angry or in conflict.

- Write your name on a piece of paper or in your journal and by your name, write what you might say to begin a conversation with that individual.

- Now write the other person's name and what you really think that person might say, not what you wish he would say. Try to imagine for just a minute how that person might think.

- Continue this written dialogue and watch what happens.

Jokes: Jokes can be great ways to make people laugh and jokes can be used as a strategy to help diffuse a tense situation. However, some jokes make fun of certain groups of people in a negative way. Help students understand when it's appropriate to laugh at certain things and when it's inappropriate to laugh. If a joke ever hurts someone's feelings, the person has crossed the line.

Kind Words: Use kind words when dealing with angry students. Some angry students have been yelled at and confronted on a daily basis. Try a little kindness. It may go a long way toward developing a possible relationship.

Logical Consequences: Logical consequences are great at showing cause and effect. For example if a student cannot get along on the playground, then he/she loses time on the playground. If a student teases others in the lunchroom, he/she may be asked to eat alone with an adult in a separate room. The real power of logical consequences is to help students realize that their behavior has consequences that are connected with their actions. A consequence of having a "silent lunch" for misbehavior on the playground may not have the power of one of the logical consequences listed above. Try logical consequences when possible.

Laugh a Little: Laughter is great medicine—especially in helping to calm down angry students. Help these students to find ways to quit being so serious and have a little fun. Fun may involve laughing over jokes, watching a funny movie, telling funny stories, etc. Help students to find a positive outlet for their frustrations and consequently to lighten up a little.

Learn About Your Anger Sequence:

1. What pushes your anger button?

2. How does it push your button?

3. How do you respond inside when your anger button is pushed?

   a. thoughts-self talk

   b. feelings/emotional arousal

   c. psychological arousal

4. How do you respond outwardly when your anger button is pushed?

5. What are the consequences for yourself and other(s) when you "lose your cool" inappropriately?

   a. What are your thoughts?

   b. What are your feelings?

   c. How do you behave?

Copied with permission from Aggressive and Violent Students by Robert Bowman, Jo Lynn Johnson, Michael Paget & Mary Thomas- Williams, copyright 1998. Youthlight, Inc. 800-209-9774.

Life Space Intervention: "Life Space Intervention" (LSI) is a therapeutic technique developed as a strategy for dealing with emotionally upset children in school settings. Wood and Long (1991)summarized this technique that was developed by Fritz Redl and David Wineman. This technique is both simple and demanding, for it does not allow for quick fixes, but rather approaches problems with a goal of personal growth and self-control for children and adolescents. When a child or adolescent is expressing emotional pain or confusion through acting out behavior the LSI may be an effective way to gain insight and teach more adaptive and pro-social skills. First you must develop trust.

Step 1: Focus on the incident

Step 2: Encourage and allow the student to talk

Step 3: Find the central issue and identify a
therapeutic or growth oriented goal

Step 4: Select a solution or alternative means of
handling the issue, based on values

Step 5: Plan how to implement the solution;
plan for success

Step 6: Prepare to resume activity

Loneliness: Loneliness can become a big issue at any age, but especially in the middle and high school years. Students may become depressed or angry and not feel that they are a part of any group. They may even feel isolated or different and end up feeling angry with other groups of friends around the school. This is obviously a difficult problem to fix. However, if you do sense that this is a problem, try to enlist the help of some friendly students to try to reach out to the lonely student. You may also want to suggest some alternative places around campus to spend lunch such as the guidance office. The important thing is to recognize that loneliness can lead to other problems like anger and depression and to try to remedy the situation before it reaches any critical stages.

Loving and Caring: Students do more for people if they perceive that they are loved and cared about by that person.

Manipulatives: Use small things that children or teenagers can squeeze when feeling angry or frustrated. Small squeeze toys or toys and clay work great for relieving frustration for young children and teenagers. Since anger is so physical, students often need something physical to do when feeling anxious or angry. A good package of manipulatives to use is *The Chill Out Bag: Anger Rx*, (2000) Chapin, S.C.: Youthlight, Inc.

Medication Do's and Don'ts: Many students in our schools are on medication and an understanding of the issues surrounding its use is critical for teachers.

Do:
• Realize that behavior and academic performance may vary from day-to-day even with medicine.

• Monitor behavior and academic performance on medication with feedback given to parents, physicians, and counselors. Use notes, phone calls, and behavioral rating scales.

• Maintain confidentiality with children on medication with peers and adults.

• Treat medication as a controlled substance. Consult school policy regarding storage and administration.

• Be watchful for any changes in behavior (i.e., insomnia, loss of appetite, constant thirst, diarrhea, nervousness, and nausea) and in academics.

• Include counseling, academic, and behavior interventions along with medicine. Medication is not the cure or a quick fix.

• Be conscious of consistent medication administration if given at school as directed by a physician. Keep the parent informed when medication supplies are running low. Do not make the child responsible for keeping up with medication availability.

• Be available to answer questions from students as related to medication and school/behavior issues.

• Always remember…be professional!

Don't:

- Expect a miracle or a perfect student following a medication intervention.

- Single out a student in front of peers or adults to get medication via the school intercom, reminders in from of class, posted notes, etc.

- Ask a student, "Did you take your medicine today?" when a difficult day is observed. (This gives the student the message that an over-reliance on medication can "fix" his/her behavior or academics.)

Reprinted with permission. Carr, Tom. (2000)131 Creative Strategies for
Reaching Children with Anger Problems. Youthlight, Inc. Chapin, S.C.

Minimize contact with the situation or person who makes you angry. For teenagers, this may mean changing your pathway to class; for younger children, it may be sitting on opposite sides of the room. Some people may just have to agree to disagree; however, it just makes sense to stay away from potentially dangerous situations.

Maximize your opportunity to coach students to make the most of anger management strategies. Enlist the help of other students to help you.

Norms: Do activities in class that help students begin to examine the norms for how others are treated.

- Ask students to watch a TV show of their choice and count how many times people are put down for the way they look, for their religious preference, for their social class, etc. Discuss the various shows that were watched and how this might affect our own ideas and values.

- Discuss times in history when people were put down for prejudicial reasons. (Examples: Jews, slaves, modern day Christians in some countries, etc.)

- Play a game to reinforce what you have discussed. Ask all students to stand up. Tell the students that you will be playing a game and that whoever is the last one standing will win a piece of candy. Randomly begin asking people to sit down because of certain physical traits. For example, all those with brown eyes, sit down because you are not in the right category to win the prize. Next, all those with blonde hair, size 5 shoes, over a certain height, etc. sit down. Continue until you have one winner. Then, ask the students how they felt about your method of choosing the "right" person. Continue the discussion by sharing how we too often assign worth based on physical characteristics.

- Discuss how students are put down on your school campus and why. How does the average student condone or not condone these actions?

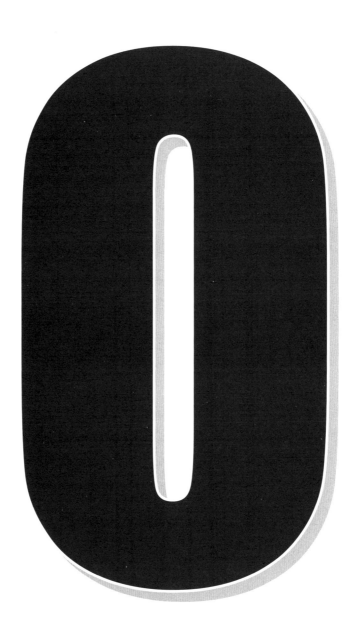

ODD: (Oppositional Defiant Disorder) is a pattern of negativistic, hostile, and defiant behavior lasting at least 6 months, during which four (or more) of the following are present:

Often:

• Loses temper

• Argues with adults

• Actively defies or refuses to comply with adults' requests or rules

• Deliberately annoys people

• Blames others for his or her mistakes or misbehavior

• Is touchy or easily annoyed by others

• Is angry and resentful

• Is spiteful or vindictive

Adapted from the Diagnostic and Statistical Manual of Mental Disorders, Fourth Edition, (1994). American Psychiatric Association. Washington, DC.

Key Intervention Tips for ODD

• Remain calm, neutral, and deliberate when following through on consequences

• Pre-plan consequences

• Understand that the student with ODD thinks you are trying to manipulate him/her.

• Provide ODD students with multiple opportunities to learn by experience…understand that this is a slow process

• Recognize that ODD students think reinforcers and consequences are attempts to control and manipulate them

• Establish good working relationships with parents

• Focus on positive goals for the ODD students

Organized Playtime: Organize games outside if you have students who are prone to get angry. Many problems occur from unstructured time with unstructured activities. Because of poor social skills, children may not know how to respond in many situations. In structured activities, the teacher can help to monitor difficult situations.

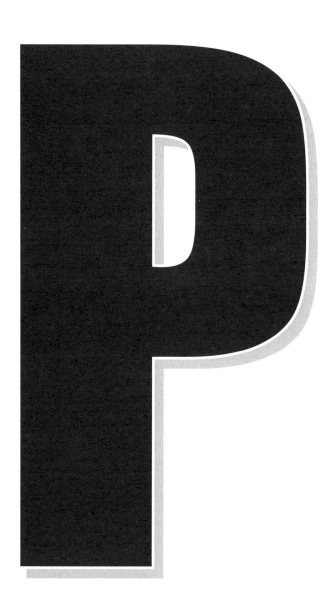

Parent Tips: How parents react to their children's anger is crucial. Adults can help defuse the anger, or they can make it worse. An important finding of the George Washington University study, is that negative parents, have a statistically stronger effect-causing bad behavior-than positive parenting has in causing good behavior. Occasionally blowing up at a child, or even a well-deserved spanking, is not going to do permanent damage. The danger is slipping into negative habits, into a pattern of negative behavior toward the child, because bad parenting is what has the strongest impact.

The next time you encounter an angry child, be careful how you REACT!

Remove the Guilt or Blame. You may not be the cause of the child's anger. You, as the teacher or parent, may be doing the best you can. Even good parents can have a difficult child. The child may have been born with a genetic tendency toward a temperament that is more moody, irritable, or short fused.

Educate Yourself. Have you learned strategies to deal with the angry child? Are you up to date on the latest research on children with ADHD, ODD, or CD? Do you use self-talk? Are you taking good care of yourself (diet, exercise, rest, etc.), that helps you cope better with stress? Do you know when to stop arguing and/or remove yourself? Are you good at recognizing anger cues?

Acknowledge/Accept the Fact that Your Child or Your Angry Student Has a Difficult Temperament/Personality. Once you accept this fact, then do the best you can to help the angry child adjust/cope with his/her emotions.

Coach, Cheerlead, and Counsel the Angry Child. Many angry students do not go willingly to anger management classes, but they react well to shorter exchanges of suggestions, ideas, and praise.

Territory Check. Monitor the child's anger outbursts, fights, and tantrums. Where are they happening? Where is the territory? Does it always happen with his/her sitter, at school, or in his/her neighborhood after school? Children placed in good territories have fewer anger problems. Keep them busy in sports, church, scouts, 4-H, etc.

Adapted from 131 Creative Strategies for Reaching Children
with Anger Problems by Tom Carr, ©2000, YouthLight, Inc.

Power Skills: Teach power skills to students to enable them to effectively deal with situations involving bullies. Some of these might include the following:

1. Stay away from bullies.

2. Travel in groups of friends.

3. Don't go to unsafe places.

4. Don't let the bullies see that they bother you.

5. Don't cry.

6. Don't act like it's any big deal.

7. Walk in the opposite direction.

8. Ask your teacher to maintain a close watch on the bully.

9. Act confident

10. Look confident

11. Watch what's going on.

12. Tell a friend what's going on. Ask them to walk with you.

13. Tell an adult if necessary.

14. Ask an adult to help you make a plan.

15. Tell them you aren't getting in trouble by fighting.

16. Tell them you don't want to get kicked out of school.

17. Tell them you know someone will catch us and I don't have time to get in trouble today.

18. Tell them in a tough way to leave you alone.

19. Stay calm

20. Keep a safe distance

21. Walk away

22. Say "Stop it"

23. Say "Leave me alone"

24. Say "Whatever"

25. Use humor

26. Use I messages.

27. If you're in danger, get out of there fast.

28. Smile mysteriously and say nothing.

29. Count to 10 under your breath while just staring at them and walking off.

30. Offer a compliment

31. Picture the rude person wearing a clown suit.

32. Walk with someone who's having problems and help them take a stand.

33. Change the subject. Ask them if they are going to the game or saw a show on TV.

34. Agree with the bully. Tell them he/she is absolutely right.

35. Keep saying no if they want something from you.

36. Act like you can't remember the bully's name.

37. Be a broken record. Keep saying the same thing over and over.

38. Anticipate what will happen and practice what you can do.

39. Tell the bully if what they're making fun of is really a medical condition.

Adapted with permission from Guidance Rocks by Kathy Cooper and Marianne Vandawalker .(2003). Youthlight, Inc. Chapin, S.C. In Press

Powerless Skills: Teach that some responses may be inappropriate to bullies because they may cause the situation to continue. Some bullies like to pick on students who show some kind of weakness. Make sure students understand how the following responses render them powerless with bullies.

1. Cry

2. Shiver

3. Act terrified

4. Hit

5. Yell

6. Kick

7. Scream

8. Hold your head down

9. Call names

10. Quit coming to school

11. Get sick every time you see the bully

12. Don't go in the cafeteria anymore

13. Don't go outside any more

14. Give the bully your lunch money

15. Let the bully copy your paper

16. Do whatever the bully says

17. Run away from home

18. Keep it all to yourself

19. Don't get around to telling your parents

20. Don't get around to telling your teachers

21. Don't get around to telling your friends

22. Continue to place yourself in dangerous situations

23. Walk by the bully every day you can

24. Try to change schools

25. Start feeling depressed all the time

26. Start letting your grades drop

27. Start feeling scared every minute of the day

28. Think no one can help you

29. Play a trick on the bully

30. Act pitiful all the time

31. Let this problem with the bully go on for a long time

Adapted with permission from Guidance Rocks by Kathy Cooper and Marianne Vandawalker (2003). Youthlight, Inc. Chapin, S.C. In Press.

Physical Activity: Some students become so angry that they need to run or do something else physical to let off a little steam. Make plans to allow students to participate in organized sports if possible. This is a great way to learn control and discipline while getting rid of a lot of pent up anger. If organized sports are not possible, allow students an opportunity to play, throw balls, shoot basketball, etc.

Play Anthropologist: Mary Pipher (1994) said that adolescent girls can be encouraged to view their culture through the eyes of an anthropologist in a strange new society. We can help them understand the parts of their culture that are helpful and those that are harmful, those they have choices about and those they don't.

Peer Listening: "The best metal detector is the student," according to Ronald Stephens of the National School Safety Center. (Time, March 19, 2001, p. 33) In 75 % of school violence incidents, the attacker told someone else. Peer Listening helps.

- Such programs focus on building relationships

- They equip young people with helping skills that offer caring, support, and guidance toward others.

- Benson (1990) noted that youth who engaged in projects and programs to help others on a weekly basis were less likely to report at-risk behaviors.

- Powell, et.al, (1996) reported that such programs resulted in modified students' self-reported attitudes about violent behavior, improved school discipline and reduced absenteeism.

- Guanci (2002) described the success of a middle school peer mediation program. Ninety-two percent of the peer mediations had successful results. Seventy-eight percent of the students felt the program was successful while 64 percent felt it had improved school climate. Also, 90 % of the students were aware there was a peer mediation program in the school. Twenty-two percent participated in it, 73 percent said they would go to a peer mediator if they had a conflict, and 89 percent understood how the program works.

Peer Mediation: Teach students a method for mediating problems between students. You may choose to have simple steps like the ones that follow:

1. Ask each student to state the problem and how he/she feels about the problem.

2. Ask each student to state what he/she believes to be an appropriate solution to the problem.

3. Ask students to determine a solution to the problem.

4. Write down the solution to the problem. Ask both students to sign this agreement.

5. Determine what might happen if the agreement is broken.

Choose a place in the room where students can work out problems, or set up times with the counselor when your students can come and mediate problems.

Paranoia: Some students think that everyone else is after them, staring at them or talking about them. Challenge this way of thinking and ask the student to provide proof of this "conspiracy" before accepting it as the truth. Challenge students to look at situations in a different way. For example, if someone looks at you while walking down the hallway, instead of thinking that this person hates the way your new pants look, how about thinking that this person may be staring in space, may actually wish he or she had a pair of pants like yours, or may not be thinking about you at all?

Prevent School Violence: Sprague and Walker (2000) summarized the following Safety Sources of Vulnerability in School Settings

School Space Issues

• Window height

• Entrances and exits (number and type)

• Bathrooms (location and design)

• Supervision patterns and adult/student ratios in supervision

• Traffic patterns

• Lighting

Leadership and Management Issues

- Effectiveness and quality

- Firm, consistent, caring discipline procedures

- Inclusive, positive school climate

- Effective home school relationships and communications

- Effective staff development and support

- Active student engagement

The Neighborhood

- Degree of safety

- Level of crime

- Access to alcohol and drugs

- Violent media access

- Availability of after school activities

The Students

- Level of poverty

- Number of at-risk students

- Arrests—type and number in the school and community

- Discipline referrals

- Levels of academic achievement

Put-ups not put-downs: Establish a no-putdowns rule for your classroom. Every time a student puts someone else down, ask the student to write a note identifying three strengths of the person who was put down. Prior to beginning this activity, ask students to give clear examples of put-downs. Do a short activity by giving random examples of positive (put-ups) and negative statements (put-downs). Ask students to stand if it's a positive statement and sit if the statement is a put-down statement.

77

Quit: Make a plan to quit doing ineffective things with anger management. Some of these may include the following:

- Quit allowing others to control you.

- Quit allowing anger to control your life.

- Quit responding to situations without thinking about the consequences.

- Quit believing that everyone is out to get you.

- Quit believing negative thoughts that you cannot prove to be true.

Rational Thinking: Learn the difference between rational and irrational thinking. Rational thinking involves thoughts that are logical and true and lead to manageable emotions. Irrational thinking involves thoughts that are illogical and untrue and lead to extreme emotions. Help children learn that their beliefs about any situation will almost always determine their emotional outcome.

For example:

1. The teacher asks you to stay inside for recess.

2. You think to yourself how the teacher is unfair and mean and is picking on you because she had your brother last year.

3. You feel angry at the teacher and about the situation. You huff and puff, eventually talk back to the teacher, and get in even more trouble.

Better solution:

1. The teacher asks you to stay inside for recess.

2. You think to yourself that you probably deserve it since this is the third time you've forgotten your homework.

3. You feel bad that you've missed recess, but decide that bringing in your homework will have to be a priority from now on.

Redirect: Redirect a student the minute you see he/she is feeling angry. Send them on an errand, send them to see the counselor, ask them to draw a picture, ask them to clean up a place in your room, ask him/her to listen to music, take a walk, etc. Your goal is to break the pattern of anger before it escalates any further.

Remove the Audience: Nothing fuels a fire like a lot of people standing around. Remember to get rid of the audience so that you can present students the opportunity to back down without feeling embarrassed in front of their friends. You might remove the audience by trying some of the following suggestions:

• Designate one student to take the class to a predetermined location.

• Designate one student to go to get someone to pick up your class.

• Ask the student to step outside to talk to you.

- Send a note to the office requesting help if you think the student is having a bad day.

- Call parents of those students who watch fights or think of some other consequences.

Research on Anger Management Programs: The 2002 anger study of fifth and sixth graders by Fryxell resulted in recommendations for anger management programs for youth.

- Family members should be included.

- Anger management and emotional control programs should be a part of pre-natal and early parenting education programs so that parents can serve as coaches for their children.

- Students at risk for chronic anger need anger prevention or emotional regulation counseling as individuals or in groups.

- All children could benefit from anger management programs that focus on social skills and building relationships. This is a proactive approach.

Resilient Students: Our goal in working with students is to help them develop resilience. According to Sullivan (2001), resilient students

- Know how to solve problems.

- Know whom to turn to for help.

- Have some sense of mastery over their lives— a sense of efficacy.

- Feel they can learn from their mistakes.

- Have a close relationship with at least one "charismatic adult," many times a teacher.

- Have been encouraged and supported by an adult to master something.

Restitution: Make sure students go this second step in making things right in an angry situation. Obviously the first step in an angry situation is to offer an apology, and the second step is to "fix it and make it better." This might involve some of the following:

- *Teasing remarks*—Writing down complimentary remarks.

- *Stealing something*—Replacing the stolen item with an equal replacement.

- *Hurting someone*—Getting the first aid kit and helping to "fix" up the person (with the person's permission).

- *Making a mess*—Cleaning up the mess.

Restitution is tied directly to the problem itself and therefore should have a greater impact on the person doing the restitution than an unrelated consequence might have on the person. Restitution has a lot to do with empathy and caring for others.

Reframing: Use this method when dealing with an angry situation. For example, when an angry student comes storming into the classroom, instead of saying "Go straight to the principal's office—You'll not come in my classroom like that," how about reframing and saying "It looks like you're really angry today. How about I get the class started and we can talk outside for a moment." Students will respond differently and you can determine what has happened to make them enter the classroom angry. Maybe their mom yelled at them, maybe another student just called them a name, or maybe he/she has a headache. You never know until you ask.

Relationships: Help adolescents define relationships. Often in boy-girl relationships, one party knows more about the other's feelings than their own and may allow the other party to define the relationship. Help them understand that it takes two strong "I's" to make a strong "We."

Remember! In dealing with angry students, we must
- Remember not to judge the student

- Remain firm but gentle

- Believe in our own skills

- Remember that if the anger is about something else, we need to deal with the something else.

- Remember that anger is normal in the early stages of trauma

- Understand that anger management works best when the student "owns his anger."

Adapted from an audio tape of Dr. Jerry Deffenbacher during the Many Faces of Anger Conference in Nashville, TN May 1999.

83

Respect: Treat students with the same respect that you would like to be treated with. Don't discount their feelings as ridiculous, even though sometimes it may be difficult to see why students become upset over some seemingly small issues. Remember that it's all about developmental stages in student's lives, and we should treat each issue like it is important because it truly is important to these students. This is a way of validating the student and his/her feelings. Many angry students feel that no one respects them.

Restrain or not Restrain? Check with your principal. What is the school or county policy on restraining children?

- Take a class on restraining and safety issues. Invite your county's Director of Exceptional Children to lead a workshop at your school to go over acceptable strategies for handling extremely violent, aggressive students.

- If a student refuses to leave the room, call the office. Don't physically force the child.

- If a child runs out of class or runs away from you, don't chase. Notify the office immediately.

- Use physical restraint for safety issues only. Is the child hurting him/herself or others?

- If for some reason you do have to hold or restrain a child, have another adult present as a witness.

- Don't restrain for compliance.

- Don't restrain if you are angry.

- Document the event.

- After the event, talk out your feelings with a co-worker.

Reprinted with permission. Carr, Tom. (2000)131 Creative Strategies for
Reaching Children with Anger Problems. Youthlight, Inc. Chapin, S.C.

Roadblocks to Anger Management: Many young people are resistant to change and believe it is acceptable to use anger for some of the following reasons. They believe:

- *Strong Anger is Justified and Appropriate.* Many students may not have been socialized to react with alternative emotions. That is, their culture, family, or peer group may not have modeled alternative emotional reactions, or they may have actually sanctioned high levels of anger. In such situations, these persons may fail to evaluate their angry reactions as deviant.

- ***Other People Are Responsible for Their Anger.*** Angry people often fail to take responsibility for their emotions; they assign responsibility for their emotions to external events. "She made me angry!"

- ***The Target of Their Anger is Not Important.*** Anger usually occurs along the belief that the target of one's anger is a totally worthless human being. Because the transgressor responsible for the person's anger is a worthless, condemnable individual, he/she deserves the angry person's wrath and must pay for the transgression.

- ***They Are Self-Righteous.*** Angry people almost always believe that they have been wronged or treated unfairly. The transgressors are portrayed as morally wrong. Angry people are rarely willing to examine their own role in an interpersonal conflict.

- ***They Believe in Cathartic Expression.*** Most angry people believe that people must release their anger. They believe that holding their anger "inside" will eventually lead to greater anger and illness, and that anger expression is healthy and necessary. Unfortunately their interpretation of "cathartic" often results in aggressive and violent behavior.

- ***They Get Short-Term Reinforcement.*** Angry people are often temporarily reinforced for their temper tantrums by significant others' compliance with the former's demands. Many angry kids end up getting what they want so they learn that anger works. Plus, fits of anger get them a lot of attention.

Reprinted with permission. Developmental Resources.(2003) Creative Strategies for Reaching Students with Anger Problems. Workshop Handout. Chapin, S.C.

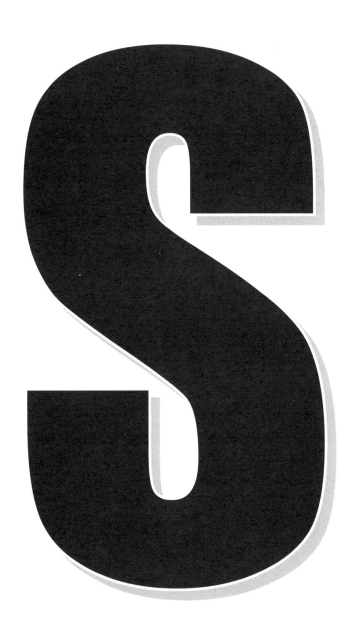

School Shooters: There Are No Stereotypes!

The U.S. Secret Service has released its finding on a study of 41 school shooters in 37 incidents. Bill Dedman (2000) with the Chicago Sun Times summarized the findings.

• Most incidents are planned in advanced many for at least two weeks to two days. Dylan Lebold in the Columbine case indicted his desire to go on a killing spree

• Almost all of the shooters had come to the attention of someone for behavior problems. The adults usually didn't investigate.

• Few of the shooters had close relationships with adults or participated in organized group activities.

• Three-fourths of the shooters told someone, usually students, of their plans, some more than one person.

• Few of the shooters had a diagnosed mental illness or histories of drug or alcohol abuse.

• However, three-fourths had a history of feeling depressed or desperate and had threatened to kill themselves. Six did so during the attack.

• The most frequent motive was revenge. In most cases, the attack was the first attempted violence against the target.

• Many felt the attack was the way to solve a problem.

• Bullying was common.

• Some had lost a love, been expelled, suspended or families were planning to move. In three-fourths of the cases, the shooters experienced difficulty dealing with a major relationship change or a loss of status.

• The shootings were not random. Some shooters had developed lists. Students, principals, or teachers could be targets. In one-half of the cases, the shootings were planned to target as many people as possible.

• Most were not considered violent students or bullies themselves and had not harmed animals.

• Six in ten showed interest in violent media and more often in their own writing,

• Weapon access was easy at home or from friends, bought legally or illegally, or stolen. Some parents gave weapons as gifts. About half had a history of gun use but for most it was not an obsession.

• Most of the shooting attacks were brief and resolved before police arrived. In these cases a students or staff member stopped the student, he stopped on his own, or killed himself. Police had to use their weapons in only three cases.

Reddy, M., Borum, R., Berglund, J., Vossekuil, B., Fein, R., & Modzeleski,(2001) in reviewing various threat assessment approaches, advocate a deductive, fact-based approach to investigate and assess the risk for targeted violence in schools. Specifically, these authors recommend the U.S. Service threat assessment approach for school administrators, mental health professionals, law enforcement personnel, and others working to maintain school safety.

This assessment involves the individual conducting the inquiry to answer questions and gather information to determine whether the student's behavior is moving toward violent action. *There is no one profile.* Instead, violence results when these factors interact: situation, perpetrator, target, and setting. Questions in the assessment concern the following:

• Motivation that led to the behavior

• Communication about intentions and ideas

• Recent losses, including loss of status

• Attack-related behaviors and planning

• Mental condition

• Whether behavior and communications are consistent

• Others' concern about the student's potential to do harm

• Ability of the student to organize and carry out a
   plan of attack

• Environmental factors that can increase the possibility
   of an attack

• Unusual interest in violence.

The data are triangulated. In other words, other sources are used such as family members, friends, classmates, teachers, school records. A synthesis of the results are used to create a risk-management plan.

The FBI suggests examining the following prongs of the life of a student who has made a threat:

Prong 1: Personality of the Student

Includes 28 personality traits such as low tolerance for frustration, poor coping skills, narcissism, dehumanization of others, exaggerated or pathological need for attention, intolerance, and fascination with violence-filled entertainment.

Prong 2: Family Dynamics

Includes six different family dynamics including turbulent parent-child relationships, the acceptance of pathological behavior, access to weapons, lack of intimacy, the domination of the home by the student, and no limits or monitoring of the child's television and Internet usage.

Prong 3: School Dynamics and the Student's Role in Those Dynamics

Includes six signs including student's attachment to school (or lack thereof), tolerance for disrespectful behavior, inequitable discipline, inflexible culture, pecking order among students, code of silence and unsupervised computer access.

Prong 4: Social Dynamics

Includes five outside influences such as media, entertainment and technology, peer groups, outside interests, drugs and alcohol and the copycat effect.

http://www.fbi.gov.

School Size: Are small schools really safer? Klonsky (2002) says yes. One in four secondary schools in the United States has more than 1000 students and it is not unusual to see enrollments of 2000 or 3000. Granted, such large high schools are more economically efficient than several small ones.

However, the 1998 report of the National Center for Educational Statistics revealed that schools of more than 1000 students are eight times more likely to report a serious violent incident than small schools (300 or less). Meier (1995) in her book *The Power of Their Ideas* described a small school in Harlem she founded – Central Park East. She said that small schools "offer what metal detectors and guards cannot: the safety and security of being known well by people who care about you" (p. 112). This is the opposite of the anonymity often experienced in large schools.

Klonsky identified the attributes of small schools:

• No more than 400 students

• Teachers and students know each other well.

• The school is a community of professionals who reflect on their practice and work together.

• Teachers tend to move with student cohorts through the years.

• Small schools often are autonomous and believe in teacher leadership

• It is easier for a small school to have a clear sense of purpose.

• Small schools are in a better position to identify and help troubled students.

• Large schools can create a "smaller feeling" through schools within schools and learning communities

Seasonal Trends in School Violence: Adams (2002) described the results of a study of the seasonal variations of school homicides and suicides between 1994 and 1999. The findings were as follows.

• Homicides peaked at semester beginnings and then tapered off. This can be a stressful time for students in forming new relationships with students and peers. There may also be grudges from holiday breaks.

• Suicides were higher in the spring—the time of proms, graduation, report cards, and final exams.

• The findings do not apply to all high profile shootings. However, the Columbine shooters also committed suicide in the spring shooting.

• Most of the school homicides involved one victim and one perpetrator. Multiple victims were found in less than 10 percent of cases.

Regardless of the season, Bowman, R.P. (2002) believes that most incidents of anger outbursts occurred during times of transition—the beginning and end of the school day as well as during lunch periods.

Secret Codes: Make a deal with another teacher complete with special "codes." If you ask a student to take over a few books, the teacher will keep the student only a few minutes. If you ask a student to take over a lot of books, the teacher will keep the student a longer time. The higher the stack of books, the longer the other teacher knows to keep the student out of the first teacher's classroom. This strategy is designed as a subtle time-out. In fact, the student would not even know that he/she is being sent to a time-out. Whenever a student is on the brink of getting into trouble, send him/her on this mission. It breaks the cycle, and gives you a break at the same time.

Stories: Use stories to tell students about both effective and ineffective ways of dealing with conflict. Literature is filled with great examples and provides an excellent teaching tool for elementary, middle, and high school students.

Stress Management: Many students get into trouble because of stress. They simply don't know how to manage stressful situations and may need to be taught. Try some of the following techniques:

- Set a time line to complete projects.

- Balance work with a little "fun" time.

- Get plenty of rest.

- Eat right.

- Stay clear of substance abuse.

- Talk to someone when feeling anxious or worried.

- Make a plan with your teacher or parent to deal with the stress.

- Watch a movie, go to the park, take a walk, talk to a friend, take a hot bath, play football, shoot some hoops, etc. when feeling stressed. Find something to do that will help you relax.

Substance Abuse Prevention Activities: Students often turn to cigarettes, drugs, or alcohol when feeling angry, stressed, or upset. If you suspect abuse, try to work with students and parents to set up appropriate counseling. Accountability measures can be set up to help parents keep a better handle on this problem. Use activities like Tom Jackson's books *Activities That Teach, More Activities that Teach, and Still More Activities That Teach* to provide active learning lessons for students.

Shadowing: If students are really angry, ask parents to come in and shadow the student for the day. The older the students get, the more embarrassed they become when parents come in. Hopefully, the positive influence of the parent coming in will become a negative reinforcer for the child's inappropriate behavior.

Suicide Prevention: Anger can sometimes be turned inward and this anger can sometimes become dangerous. If students write or talk about suicide in any way, take it seriously. Call parents, suggest counseling, and make a plan to help this student.

Snap Out of It: If you are being grumpy and can control it, just watch what you're doing and snap out of it and as quickly as possible. We all feel aggravated some days and just have to control this effectively until we're over this negative feeling. This might mean keeping your mouth closed, not going around people who aggravate you, and trying to manage your stress until you get in a better mood. Most of us can make appropriate choices and control our anger on most days. So, when you can, just snap out of it by doing something positive and dealing with the situation in a positive way.

Social Skills: Many students are lacking in social skills and simply do not know how to play or talk with others. Some students may spend a lot of time alone or on the computer and may be inexperienced in sharing with others or playing with large groups of children. Social skills groups are effective ways to teach students simple skills that will help them in certain situations.

Staying Cool: Kolman (2000) developed these terms to use with angry students.

> *Sparks*—Sparks are those things that set us off or make us angry—a friend takes a toy away or Mom says you have to clean your room before you go to a friend's house.

> *Clues*—Clues are body signs that help us know when we become mad or angry—a stomachache, a headache, clenched fist, red face or tears.

> *Anger Blasters*—Anger Blasters are things we do to calm ourselves down—taking a walk, riding a bike, punching a pillow, giving yourself a timeout, or talking with someone you trust.

> *People Skills*—People Skills are used to solve the problems that make us angry—listening to the other person and not interrupting, looking that person in the eye and using positive body language.

Anger Control Checks—Anger Control Checks are what we use to grade ourselves on how well we controlled our anger. For example:

"I know what my spark and my clues were. That's great! Because if I know I'm angry, I can do something about it. Next time, I'll be able to use 'good power' to stop myself from blowing up."

"On a scale of one to 10, I give myself a five. I blew up, but then gave myself a timeout. Better late than never, but I could have done much better."

Source: How to stay cool when a storm brews. Asheville Citizen-Times August 20, 2000, p. B3

Symptom Prescription: Molnar and Lindquist (1989) developed a paradoxical strategy and it should be used very cautiously. In this strategy, you actually give permission for the child to continue the behavior in a prescribed fashion. Obviously, you do not want the behavior to continue—hence the paradox. It's often just not as "fun" to continue a behavior when you have permission to do it. For example:

• *Throwing spit balls*—Why don't you stay in during recess and throw spitballs for 15 minutes? It will help develop your arm for baseball practice.

• *Temper tantrums*—Why don't you go ahead and have the tantrums? But we'd like to schedule them for 10:00 and 12:00 because we have extra time then.

• *Pencil tapping*—Go ahead and tap your pencils while I talk. It will give me a little background beat for my talk.

Shame: Some anger arises because people are very ashamed about a particular issue. For example, if another student picks on them about their mom, their house, their size, their nose, their way of talking, etc, it could open a very sensitive area and students could respond by fighting to protect themselves. Sometimes, this kind of problem might involve having an adult get involved to stop the other students from being so insensitive and also helping the angry student deal with whatever the underlying problem is.

Stress Reliever Games: The following activities are stress releasing activities which can be done individually while sitting at a desk

- *Lemon Game for Lemonade (K-4)*

  Hold your arms out in front of you. Close and clinch your fists as if you are holding onto two lemons to squeeze for making lemonade. Count to 12 and release.

- *Elephant Game (K-12)*

  Sit up straight and hold your stomach in tightly. Pretend you are getting ready for an elephant at the circus to step on your stomach. Count to 12 and release.

- *Cat Stretching Game (K-12)*

  Hold your arms and legs straight out in front of you. Point your toes to the sky and stretch as a cat does. Count to 12 and release.

- *Turtle Game(K-4)*

  Hold your shoulders up to your ears and count to 12 and release.

- *Plant a Garden (K-4)*

  Choose a partner. Ask your partner to face your back. Ask them to be a gardener and turn your back into the garden. Ask the gardener to

  —Till the soil by using their hands to rub your back.

  —Plant the seeds by twisting their fingers into your back.

  —Rake the soil to cover the seeds by running their fingers down your back.

  —Water the soil by using trickling or gentle pounding motions.

  —Weed the garden by using easy pinching motions

  —Pick the fruit by using large hand motions.

  —Till all the plants under by using large up and down movements with your hand.

Used with permission from Guidance Rocks by Kathy Cooper and Marianne Vandawaller. (2003) Youthlight, Inc. In Press

Transition Tickets: Many difficult situations may arise as a result of unstructured time in or out of the classroom or during periods of transition. Some students may become frustrated from the high level of activity, the lack of organization, his/her own lack of social skills, or the inability to work with groups of children. Work out a plan with a student for these times. You may want to give the children specific jobs during these times and use transition tickets as rewards for a student during times he/she does not get in trouble. Upon collection of a certain number of tickets, the student might achieve a reward that you have predetermined.

Adapted from 131 Creative Strategies for Reaching Children
with Anger Problems by Tom Carr, ©2000, YouthLight, Inc.

Time Out: Work out specific places that an angry student might go to calm down and get away. These might include a quiet place in your room where the child can draw, listen to music, or put together a puzzle. It might be a fellow teacher's room, a counselor's office, or some other designated place in the school. Use your own judgment as to what might work the best with particular children.

Time In: Teach the student the concept of "Time In," the responsibility after time out to come back and deal with the issue. The student may need to role play or write what he or she needs to say to the teacher.

Thinking vs. Feeling: Teach adolescents to separate thinking from feeling. How do I feel about this vs. what do I do about this?

Talk about the Problem: Not in the heat of the anger, but after a student has calmed down, offer him/her an opportunity to talk about what happened. Most students will readily talk after the fact. At this time, you can discuss what made you angry and make a plan for what you can do differently next time.

Talk in a Friendly Voice: If someone is bothering you, you can merely ask him/her to leave you alone in a friendly voice.

Talk in a Firm Voice: If someone is bothering you and talking in a friendly voice does not work, you can talk firmly to the other person and ask him/her to leave you alone. At this time, you may offer a consequence of reporting the situation to an adult if it does not get better.

Touch: The Three H's—High Five, Handshake, Hug. Many students respond to touch but some school districts have strict rules about touching students. Dr. Robert Bowman who created this strategy suggested that alternatives include greeting each student by name, shaking hands, or letting the child hug a hand puppet.

Trifold Plan: A good activity to stimulate "owning one's anger" and taking action to do something about it.

  • Have the student take a piece of paper and fold it like a letter going into an envelope.

  • Open it up and turn it sideways

  • On the left panel, draw three different things that make you angry.

  • On the right panel, list 3 of your personal strengths.

  • On the middle panel, draw links between your strengths and things that push your buttons and write how you will use those strengths.

Turtles: Younger students may like the analogy of the turtle going into his shell as a visual reminder of how to deal with anger. You might suggest that turtles go into their shell when they are anxious, fearful, or in need of protection. Likewise, we might find a place to be alone to figure out how we need to deal with a situation. The answers to the problem may include getting someone else to help or simply dealing with the problem on our own. Ultimately, the purpose of going into our shell is to find a way to step back from the problem to make a plan before acting impulsively.

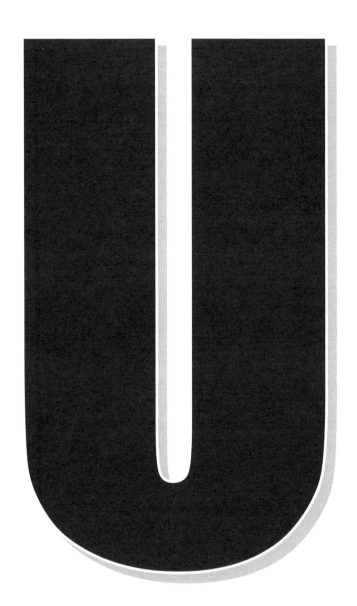

Understanding the Problem: Take time to understand where the problem resulting in anger is coming from. Is it…

• Frustration because of a learning problem?

• Disappointment because of a relationship with a parent?

• Anxiety because of abuse in the home?

• Fear because of excessive bullying from a classmate?

• An attempt to achieve power because of a feeling of powerlessness?

• An attempt to fight back because others constantly are making fun of you because of being different in some way?

Before you can prescribe a solution, you must know the problem. Prescribing the same solution for anger is about as effective as prescribing the same medication for every medical problem. Solutions must be tailored to each student and each problem individually.

Violence Prevention: Watch your school for potentially violent students and make plans to deal with them. Sometimes this is as simple as making a plan for anger management with the student; sometimes it is as complicated as making arrangements for them to go to another school. Remember, it's not only the students who are angry on the outside that we need to worry about but also the depressed student, the lonely student, the isolated student, the picked on student, and the anxious student. These students may need to be referred to the counselor and the counselor can make appropriate referrals, make appropriate plans, or make arrangements for the students to have jobs in the school to feel more connected.

Venting: Teach students how to vent appropriately by walking away, talking about the problems, squeezing balls, running, shooting hoops, getting away from the problem, etc. Self-control is very necessary in keeping students out of trouble.

Writing Works! Recent studies have validated the use of writing as an effective means of dealing with stressful events. The April 14, 1999 issue of *The Journal of the American Medical Association* reported results of a State University of New York study. Findings indicated that writing was beneficial for those who suffer with asthma and arthritis, which can both be triggered by stress. The article also described Pennebaker's study at the University of Texas at Austin on college freshmen that revealed that writing as a cathartic approach dulled the emotional impact of an experience and helped an individual confront it.

Important Reminder:

Teachers or others who work with writing activities should issue a disclaimer to students concerning confidentiality. It helps to say something like this, "You may write anything you wish and I will keep it confidential but please understand that if you should write something that would lead me to believe that harm may come to you or others, I would need to bring this to the attention of someone who could help you.

X out violence: X out violence by doing things that build you up. Some examples might be:

- Becoming involved on a sports team.

- Participating in church youth activities

- Joining clubs at school

- Joining a musical group

- Being a part of 4-H

- Joining the scouts

- Reading books

- Exercising daily

- Watching good things on TV

- Finding a service project

- Helping others

- Learning to do something new

The best way to quit being "mean" to people is to start being "nice" to other people and yourself. You'll not only stay out of trouble, but feel really good about yourself.

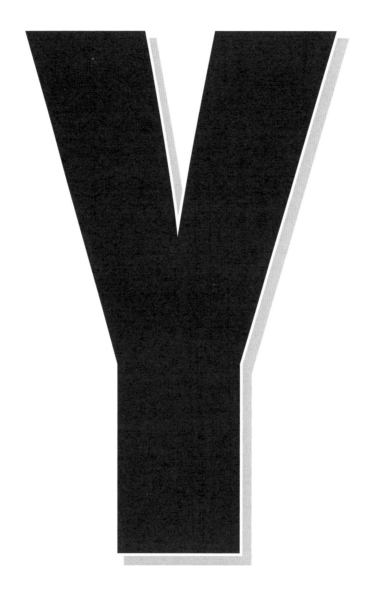

Yelling is Out: Remember people who yell at each other rarely accomplish anything. Usually a yelling situation becomes a lose-lose situation, and both people end up saying things they wish they had not. When the situation gets to this level, just walk away and continue the discussion later when both people are calmed down.

Zip it Up: Just keep your mouth closed when you're angry if you know you'll say things you shouldn't. Remember the old saying, "If you can't say something nice, don't say anything at all." While you may sometimes have to talk about unpleasant things, you need to do this when you're most in control of your words. This way you can accomplish the most good. People will turn you off if you are aggressive in your tone and hateful with your words. So, zip it up until you're in control and can say what you really mean.

Adams, J. (2002). Seasonal trends in school violence. *Psychology Today.* 35,128.

Alexander, C. (2002). Helping high school counselors cope with violence. *USA Today Magazine.* 130, 52-53.

Beane, A. (1999). *The bully free classroom.* Minneapolis: Free Spirit Publishing.

Benson, P. (1990). *The troubled journey: a portrait of 6th-12th grade youth.* Minneapolis: Search Institute

Berry, L. ((1994). Dealing with aggressive students on the spot. *Education Digest. 60,* 27-29.

Black, J. & English, F. (1986). *What they don't tell you in schools of education about school administration.* Lancaster, PA: Technomic Publishing Co.

Bowman, D. (2001). Federal study stresses warning signs of school violence. *Education Week. 21,* 12.

Bowman, R. (2002). Personal Interview.

Breunlin, D., Cimmarusti, R., Bryant-Edwards, T., & Hetherington, J. (2002). Conflict resolution training as an alternative to suspension for violent behavior.*The Journal of Educational Research. 95,* 349-357

Bushman, B., Baumeister, R., & Stack, A. (1999). "Catharsis, Aggression, and Persuasive Influence: Self-fulfilling or Self-defeating Prophecies?" *Journal of Personality and Social Psychology. 76,* 367-76.

Carr, T. (2000). *131 creative strategies for reaching children with anger problems.* Chapin, SC: Youthlight, Inc.

Cloud, J., Cole, W., Thigpen, D., Harbart, N., Healy, R., Jackson, D., McDowell, J., Roche, T. & Winters, R. (2001). The Legacy of Columbine. *Time. 157,* 32-36.

Cooper, K. & Vandawalker, M. (1997) *Power Play.* Chapin, SC: Youthlight, Inc.

Cooper, K. & Vandawalker, M. (2003). *Guidance Rocks.* Chapin, SC: Youthlight, Inc. In Press.

Dedman, B. (2000). Deadly lessons school shooters tell. *Chicago Sun Times Exclusive Report.* October 15-16.

Dedman, B. (2000). Tips on Listening to Boys. *Chicago Sun Times Exclusive Report.* October 15-16.

Fay, J. & Funk, A. (1998). *Teaching with love and logic: taking control of the classroom.* Golden, Colorado: The Love and Logic Press.

Frankel, F. (1996) *Good friends are hard to find.* Glendale, CA.: Perspective Publishing.

Fryxell, D. (2000). Personal, social and family characteristics of angry students. *Professional School Counseling. 4,* 86-94.

Glasser, W. (1998). *Choice theory.* New York: Harper Collins.

Glasser, W. (1986). *Control theory in the classroom.* New York: Harper and Row.

Goleman, (1995). *Emotional intelligence.* New York: Harper & Row.

Gossen, D. (1992). *Restitution.* Chapel Hill: New View Publications.

Greene, R. (2001). *The explosive child.* New York: Harper Collins.

Guanci, J. (2002). Peer mediation: a winning solution of conflict resolution. *Education Digest. 67,* 26-33.

"How to stay cool when a storm brews," *Asheville Citizen Times,* August 20, 2000, B3.

Jackson, T. (1993) *Activities that teach.* Cedar City: Red Rock Publishing.

Jackson, T. (1995) *More activities that teach.* Cedar City: Red Rock Publishing.

Jackson, T. (2001). *Still more activities that teach.* Minneapolis: Educational Media Corporation.

Jones, F. (1987). *Positive classroom discipline.* Santa Cruz, CA: Fredric H. Jones & Associate, Inc.

Kassinove, H.(1995), *Anger Disorders.* Washington, DC: Taylor & Francis Publishing.

Klonsky, M. (2002), How smaller schools prevent school violence. *Educational Leadership.* 59, 65-69.

Meier, D. (1995) *The power of their ideas: lessons for America from a small school in Harlem.* Boston: Beacon Press.

Mendler, A. (1992). *How to achieve discipline with dignity in the classroom.* Bloomington, Indiana: National Education Service.

Messer, M. (2001). *Managing anger: a handbook of proven techniques.* Chicago: Anger Institute.

Messer, M. (2000). *Anger intelligence: an introduction to anger therapy.* Chicago: Anger Institute.

Molnar, A., Lindquist, B. (1989, 1990) *Changing problem behavior in schools.* San Francisco: Jossey-Bass Publishers.

Pace, M. (2002) "Bullying," *The Journal of the American Medical Association*. Vol. 285, 2132, 2156.

Pipher, M. (1994) *Reviving Ophelia: Saving the selves of adolescent girls*. New York: Putnam.

Potter-Efron, R. (1994). *Angry all the time*. Oakland: New Harbinger, Inc.

Potter-Efron, R. & Potter-Efron, P. (1995) *Letting go of anger. Oakland:* New Harbinger, Inc.

Powell, K., Muir-McClain, L. & Halasyamani, L. (1996) A review of selected school based conflict resolution and peer mediation projects. *Peer Quarterly Facilitator, 13*, 31-38.

Price, J., Telljohann, S., Dake, J., Marsico, L., Zyla, C. (2002). Urban elementary students' perceptions of fighting behavior and concerns for personal safety. *Journal of School Health. 72*,184-191.

Reddy, M., Borum, R., Berglund, J., Vossekuil, B., Fein, R., & Modzeleski, W. (2001). Evaluating risk for targeted violence in schools: comparing risk assessment, threat assessment, and other approaches. *Psychology in the Schools. 38,* 157-172.

Sprague, J. & Walker, H. (2000) Early identification and intervention for youth with antisocial and violent behavior. *Exceptional Children. 66,* 367-379.

Turecki, S. (1989) *The difficult child*. New York: Bantam.

U.S. Department of Education & U.S. Secret Service (2002). *Threat assessment in schools: a guide to managing threatening situations and creating safe school climates*. Jessup, MD: Education Publications Center.

U.S. Secret Service and U.S. Department of Education (2002). *The final report and findings of the Safe School Initiative: initial implications for the prevention of school attacks in the U.S.* Jessup, MD: Education Publications Center.

Vossekuil, B., Fein, R., Reddy, M., Borum, R. & Modzeleski, W. (2002). *The final report and findings of the Safe School Initiative: Implications for the prevention of school attacks in the United States.* Washington, D.C.: United States Secret Service and United States Department of Education.

Willert, H. (2002) Do sweat the small stuff: stemming the violence. *American Secondary Education. 30,* 2-13

Wiseman, R. (2002). *Queen bees and Wannabees.* Girls, Inc.

Wood, & Long (1991) *Life space intervention: Talking with children and youth in crisis.* Austin: Pro Ed.

About the Authors

nna T. McFadden, Ph.D. is a former high school teacher, assistant principal and principal. She was runner-up for South Carolina Teacher of the year and twice named Best Principal in a reader's poll sponsored by The State newspaper. Now an Associate Professor of Educational Leadership at Western Carolina University, she trains future principals and superintendents. She was the 2003 winner for the College of Education and Allied Professions' Botner Award for superior teaching. Anna is also the author of *Speak Softly and Carry Your Own Gym Key: A Female High School Principal's Guide to Survival* (Corwin Press) as well as articles and chapters on school leadership. She speaks around the nation on the subject of angry students.

athy Cooper, M.S.W. is currently a high school counselor in Union, North Carolina. She previously worked as an elementary school counselor and social worker, and she has been an innovator in the development of creative activities, strategies, and games that enable students to more effectively deal with problem situations in their lives. Kathy has presented seminars in more than 25 states and is the co-author of *Power Play, Quality Times for Quality Kids, Innovative Strategies for Unlocking Difficult Children, Innovative Strategies for Unlocking Difficult Adolescents,* and *Ready Freddy.*